RAINBOW OF MYSTERIES

NORMAN HABEL

Rainbow of Mysteries

MEETING THE SACRED IN NATURE

CopperHouse

Editor: Ellen Turnbull
Cover and interior design: Verena Velten
Book production: Katherine Carlisle
Proofreader: Dianne Greenslade

CopperHouse is an imprint of Wood Lake Publishing, Inc. Wood Lake Publishing acknowledges the financial support of the Government
of Canada, through the Book Publishing Indus-
try Development Program (BPIDP) for its publishing activities. Wood Lake Publishing
also acknowledges the financial support of the Province of British Columbia through
the Book Publishing Tax Credit.

At Wood Lake Publishing, we practise what we publish, being guided by a concern
for fairness, justice, and equal opportunity in all of our relationships with employees
and customers. Wood Lake Publishing is committed to caring for the environment
and all creation. Wood Lake Publishing recycles, reuses, and encourages readers to
do the same. Resources are printed on 100% post-consumer recycled paper and more
environmentally friendly groundwood papers (newsprint), whenever possible. A per-
centage of all profit is donated to charitable organizations.

Library and Archives Canada Cataloguing in Publication

Habel, Norman C.
      Rainbow of mysteries : meeting the sacred in nature / Norman Habel.

Includes index.
ISBN 978-1-77064-441-0

      1. Nature--Religious aspects--Christianity. I. Title.

BR115.N3H32 2012   261.8'8   C2012-902677-8

Published by CopperHouse
An imprint of Wood Lake Publishing Inc.
9590 Jim Bailey Road, Kelowna, BC, Canada, V4V 1R2
www.woodlakebooks.com
250.766.2778

Printing 10 9 8 7 6 5 4 3 2 1
Printed in Canada by Houghton Boston

Dedication

In memory
of my ancestors,
Wends,
who first lived in the forests
and then on farms,
loving Earth
from the day of their birth.

Contents

PREFACE 9

INTRODUCTION

The Adventure of Exploring Mystery 13

CHAPTER ONE

Red – The Mystery of Presence 33

CHAPTER TWO

Orange – The Mystery of Being Earth-Born 53

CHAPTER THREE

Gold – The Mystery of Wonder 77

CHAPTER FOUR

Green – The Mystery of Life 97

CHAPTER FIVE

Blue – The Mystery of Voice 119

CHAPTER SIX

Indigo – The Mystery of Wisdom 139

CHAPTER SEVEN

Violet – The Mystery of Compassion 163

CONCLUSION – A Rainbow Blessing 181

APPENDIX 1
Workshops for Sharing Earth Spirituality and Earth Mission 185

APPENDIX 2
Seven Rites for Exploring Mystery in Nature 191

BIBLIOGRAPHY 233

INDEX 235

Preface

In this book, I explore seven spiritual dimensions of nature
– dimensions I have come to appreciate as mysteries – and
describe how I meet the sacred in nature.

Because of my background, I tend to begin my explorations with Scripture that resonates with each mystery.
But this book is not a biblical theology or an ecological
commentary.

I am aware of my Lutheran theological heritage and its
influence on how I have related to nature in the past. This
book, however, is not a contemporary theology, although
it may inform a potential eco-theology. While this exploration may be of interest to progressive Christians, my focus
is not really on a re-interpretation of the Christian tradition. This volume is about spirituality in nature, rather than
Christianity and creation.

I identify myself now as an Earth being, and not simply
as a human being. Earth is my mother, my primal parent,
and the Christian church my adoptive parent (as I explain
in chapter 2). This position does not mean I reject my adoptive parent, but that I seek to understand my spiritual connection with my primal parent.

I begin by exploring the mystery of Presence permeating our planet. I seek to discern the Wonder that evokes

wonder in us and in nature. I investigate the mystery of Impulse that initiates life, and the rarely appreciated mystery of Wisdom encoded within the laws and rhythms of nature. I listen for the Voices of Earth, a mystery we humans tend not to hear. Finally, I ask my ultimate question: Is there Compassion in the cosmos?

Throughout these explorations, I acknowledge not only my biblical and religious backgrounds, but also confess to being "converted," as it were, by the radical insights of an ecological worldview. Ultimately, however, my spiritual connections with nature are grounded in personal experiences, moments when I meet the sacred in nature. Through these experiences, I came home to Earth. I now celebrate her spirit.

Meeting the Sacred

When a mystery
breaks the surface of nature
my consciousness quivers.
I meet the sacred,
sense the spiritual,
and wonder.

When a mystery
rises from the depths of nature
my mind seeks wisdom.
I meet the sacred,
discern the spiritual,
and wonder.

When a mystery
reveals its presence in nature
my spirit is startled.
I meet the sacred,
celebrate the spiritual,
and wonder.

Introduction
The Adventure of Exploring Mystery

That which is far off and deep,
very deep; who can find it? (Ecclesiastes 7:24)

I sat on a hill looking out to sea. (Strange how it's always "out" to sea and "in" land!) In the distance lay that elusive line we call the horizon, the seeming edge of Earth. My eye wandered along it – the brink of the planet, my home.

Above the shore, a pelican floated, calm and fearless. The horizon line for her was a little further out – just a little. A hawk fluttering even higher could eye that same line, if he chose, even further out. And so on *ad infinitum!*

That line, the edge of Earth, keeps moving away as we draw closer or fly higher. At that edge, it seems to me, the infinite and the finite merge. And this place of merger speaks to me of mystery, of the sacred in nature, and stirs within me the urge to explore the deep spirituality of Earth and the mysteries of nature.

In recent years I have written books and studies on many aspects of how we might relate to nature, creation, and the environment. I initiated *The Season of Creation*, which is concerned with how we might celebrate *with* creation rather than simply say thanks for creation. I worked with a team of scholars to develop the principles employed in *The Earth Bible* series. I have completed a critical ecological reading of Genesis 1–11, the first volume in *The Earth Bible Commentary* series. I have promoted the idea that churches need to engage in an eco-mission, what I call the Third Mission of the Church. I have even dared to distinguish between "green" and "grey" texts of the Bible in a volume entitled *An Inconvenient Text*.

Now, in my ninth decade, I believe it is time to be more personal and enunciate how I, after all these years of academic endeavour, actually connect with nature spiritually. After reading and writing tomes that have analysed biblical text from critical, social, environmental, and theological points of view, I now ask myself where, how, and why I am spiritually interconnected simultaneously with selected texts, natural contexts, and personal experiences. In other words, what mysteries in nature resonate with me at the end of my life? Can I now read the sacred text of nature, the landscape of life on this planet? Can I discern Presence in that sentient domain my fellow humans call country? If I did, what would I discover about God, life, and myself? I have lived my life reading the Scriptures to discern dimensions of God. Can I now do the same as I read nature and hear her response?

Earth spirituality is a topic close to my heart – and even closer to my spirit. I could, of course, write a theology of creation with a sub-section entitled "Theology of Earth." Such an exercise, while extremely valuable, is likely to be written from the head rather than the heart, a work in tune with the mind rather than the spirit, a venture that is theological rather than spiritual.

By exploring the spirituality of nature, I believe I am more likely to connect with the deep searchings that move the soul and the heart of the reader. This approach will, I hope, enable more readers to follow me on my spiritual journey home to Earth, my natural mother.

The Aboriginal people of Australia have the capacity to read the landscape, to experience Presence in sacred sites, to celebrate the mystery of specific locations, to trace sacred song-lines across the country, and to feel the pulses of Earth. Their capacity to read the landscape and feel its spirit is related to their sense of the land as a sentient domain and their spiritual kinship with it. As my mentor George Rosendale told me:

> Aboriginal culture is spiritual. I am spiritual. Inside of me is spirit and land, both given to me by the Creator Spirit. There is a piece of land in me and it keeps drawing me back like a magnet to the land from which I came. Because the land, too, is spiritual!

This land owns me. One piece of land that I can claim a spiritual connection with – a connection between me and the land – is the piece of land under the tree where I was born, the place where my mother buried the afterbirth and umbilical cord. The spiritual link with that piece of land goes back to the ancestors in the Dreaming. This is both a personal and a sacred connection – between the land, me and my ancestors (Rainbow Spirit Elders, 1997, 12).

How might I too learn to read the landscape, interpret nature with new eyes and ears, and meet the sacred(?)in the mysteries of the cosmos? How might I feel the spiritual magnet of Earth drawing me back to my primal home?

I do not claim that what I have discovered in this journey is unique to me. Many fellow travellers in my tradition will, I believe, also celebrate similar findings, even if they have not had the courage to reveal them. My experiences, connected as they are with biblical texts and natural contexts, will no doubt ring a bell with many of you who have searched for your place beyond the four walls of church, house, or office.

So I invite you to join me on this journey to connect with creation spiritually. I have called this experiment a *Rainbow of Mysteries*. Why? Because, in the Flood narrative, the rainbow was witness to the covenant promise of the Creator to never again destroy Earth with flood waters. The rainbow served to remind God of God's bond and divine connection with Earth and all of creation. My rainbow, following the precedent of the Creator, represents my covenant promise to explore my bonds with Earth, my spiritual connections with creation. I invite you to do the same.

My aim in this book is to explore where and how you and I might resonate with the spiritual in creation, meet the sacred in nature, and live as Earth's spiritual partner. In this book, I expose more of my soul and my spiritual world than in past writings, and these personal connections with the mysteries of creation often help to reveal the spiritual import of some texts for the first time.

The steps for my exploration of mystery in nature can be expressed in terms of the following process.

Step 1
Explore rich Bible texts
where a given mystery is still
alive and inviting

Step 2
Face how this mystery
may have been suppressed in my
Christian tradition

Step 3
Explore how the mystery in
nature is discerned through the
lens of ecology

Step 4
Explore where I, in my personal
experience, have met the sacred
in the mysteries of nature

Step 5
Discern the wisdom needed to
sustain mystery and the sacred
in nature

Step 1

Explore Bible texts where a given mystery
is still alive and inviting.

My starting point is the treasury of mysteries imbedded in the Bible. Are there texts relating to creation with which I still resonate spiritually, not because they reveal a particular eternal truth about God but because they are in tune with my spirit as an Earth being, or my deep personal experience of nature? Are there passages that suggest ways in which I might read nature ecologically and spiritually, as I have read the Scriptures?

I begin with the Bible because I have been interpreting that ancient book for more than 60 years. During that period I have employed almost every critical tool for interpretation that scholars have devised. In recent times, I have encouraged readers to interpret the Bible from an ecological perspective; that is, from the perspective of Earth and Earth community. In a recent volume entitled *An Inconvenient Text*, I even sought to establish criteria that might enable us to distinguish between those texts in the Bible that are "green" and those that are "grey." Green texts are those where humans and/or God value nature; grey texts are those where humans and/or God devalue nature.

I now want to take another step in my journey as an interpreter. Rather than explore what the Bible presents on a given topic, I plan to discover those moments where some being, voice, or element in the Bible connects with nature in a spiritual way. I am seeking moments when Earth beings – human or non-human – resonate with the spiritual in nature.

My approach will not be arbitrary and idiosyncratic, but will reflect a close literary reading of the passage under consideration, taking into account the nuances of the original languages. I will pose the following questions as part of the process of interpretation.

* How is the specific spiritual mystery in nature described, according to the orientation of the narrator?
* How do the participants in the text, whether human or other-than-human members of Earth community or Earth herself, respond to the mystery, according to the account of the narrator?
* How might these mysteries, from the cosmology of a distant world, resonate with me or my contemporaries in the current ecological and spiritual context?
* How does sensitivity to these mysteries motivate me to find ways of sustaining the mysteries of this planet and to make a covenant that will induce me to bond with Earth?

My task is to find ways of connecting with the mystery of the text in order to make it relevant, rich, and meaningful for people in a world of environmental crises and spiritual diversity. My approach throughout this exploration will be consistent with ecological hermeneutics, a methodology

I developed that enables us to identify with Earth or the Earth community and retrieve their voices in the text (Habel, 2008). Nevertheless, this journey is a new adventure, not a recapitulation of my past methodologies. After long experiments involving the reading of biblical text using a range of scholarly techniques, I also now seek ways of reading the mysteries of nature so that I may connect with the spiritual in nature.

Many of the texts I refer to are analysed by William Brown in his work *The Seven Pillars of Creation* (2010) – the title might seem to anticipate mine. I applaud his goal of relating the "ecology of wonder" to the biblical texts in question. My goal, however, is to read the biblical text from an ecological perspective and explore the spiritual dimensions of nature afresh in the light of ecology and personal spiritual experiences.

Step 2

Face how this mystery may have been suppressed in my Christian tradition.

My turning point is a re-reading of mystery in my tradition. Has my tradition – that of an Australian Lutheran – sometimes been a barrier to my connecting with nature personally? Has the Christian tradition I inherited separated me from the so-called material universe rather than inviting me to connect with creation spiritually? Has the message from the pulpit hindered me from hearing the songs and stories of nature?

This analysis has led me to rethink the way in which Christian theology, mission, and worship have understood a particular mystery in the Bible, in nature, and in life. In Christian theology, the underlying dualism that we have inherited has led to the separation of the spiritual from the material, God from creation, spirit from matter, and soul from body. In this tradition, nature has not generally been connected with the spiritual or Spirit, but devalued as simply material. While Spirit may be affirmed as a force that animates Earth, Earth is not viewed as being alive with Spirit, or sacred.

When we read from the perspective of Earth and Earth community, we discover new dimensions and relationships not only in the biblical tradition but also in the traditions of the church. By recognising an alternative cosmology to the dualistic structure that dominates our past theology, we may discover a new range of mysteries that challenge and stimulate our faith. By exploring the web of creation as a spiritual reality alive with mysteries, we may be able to discover dimensions of nature that have been ignored or suppressed in the past.

Our worship, likewise, has been conditioned by a focus on the mysteries associated with our liturgical tradition. And that tradition tends to suggest that the spiritual is linked with worship in the church and with the mysteries associated with sacraments such as baptism and the Eucharist. Christ is also believed to be present with the people of God in the church. Any suggestion that nature is a spiritual domain appropriate as a worship context or worship partner tends to be ignored. Any proposal that other domains of creation may also be sacraments is identified as false doctrine. Any consideration that we explore mystery as an integral component of our living planet and that we worship together with the natural world has been viewed with suspicion, in spite of passages such as Psalm 148.

It is time, I believe, to rethink the presence of the spiritual in nature and of mystery in each and every domain of Earth. It is time to re-read our biblical and Christian traditions, and to begin reading the landscape of our planet, and listening to the voices emerging from the sentient worlds we walk among.

Step 3

Explore how the mystery in nature is discerned through the lens of ecology.

My critical point is the challenging mystery presented by ecology. Is ecology but another academic discipline I must consider, or is ecology, as it is now understood, more like a revolutionary worldview that challenges my past understandings of how I relate to nature and, indeed, to the whole cosmos? Is my ecological conversion a new lens for reading the mysteries that surround me day and night? Is ecology, perhaps, even more radical than evolution for interpreting our natural world?

Initially, ecology was understood by many as an objective science designed to analyse the interconnected ecosystems of the universe. And that process remains fundamental to the nature of ecology. In recent years, however, ecology has revealed dimensions to the cosmos, and especially to our planet, that I believe are as readily named mysteries as the mysteries of the Bible. Scholars like Thomas Berry have begun to articulate, for example, the mystery of Earth as a community of communicating beings and entities.

> In reality there is a single integral community of the Earth that includes all its component members whether human or other than human. In this community every being has its own role to fulfil, its own dignity, its inner spontaneity. Every being has its own voice. Every being declares itself to the entire universe. Every being enters into communion with other beings. This capacity for relatedness, for presence to other beings, for spontaneity in action, is a capacity possessed by every mode of being throughout the entire universe. So too every being has rights to be recognised and revered (Berry, 1999, 4).

Earth is not a lifeless ball of stardust, but a vibrant community of presences and powers that interact and communicate with each other. All of Earth's components, from the mountains to the forests, from the oceans to the ice caps, are part of a complex living entity called Earth. And we humans, along with all other living beings, are privileged to be an integral part of this living planet. Earth provides the habitat where all consciousness, including spiritual awareness, is nurtured. We have become acutely aware that Earth is not a collection of separate continents or discrete domains isolated by geographical or geological barriers. We now realise that Earth is one amazing domain where all components are connected in a wondrous web. What happens in the ocean currents in one region influences life on a distant shore. What happens in a desert storm influences life in a rain forest.

The contemporary environmental crisis, however, has made us realise that Earth systems are fragile. Human beings have the capacity to upset the balance of forces that govern the life of the planet. The balancing of Earth's impulses is a mystery. The delicate patterns of pulses that permeate Earth leave us wondering in amazement. To explore the balancing of Earth's systems is tantamount to an adventure of faith.

In our new cosmology, with our ecology-informed view of the natural world, and more particularly of Earth, I would suggest that as we read we are conscious of Earth

* as a living planet that originated in cosmos space and evolved into a living habitat, where each entity interacts with other entities by virtue of its inner drive to exist;
* as a fragile web of interconnected and interdependent forces and domains of existence that form a complex community of worth and wonder;
* as a living community in which humans and all other organisms are kin who live, move, communicate, and have a common destiny.

The current ecological cosmology challenges us to read text, tradition, and nature from within Earth as our habitat, with Earth as our partner, and with concern for a suffering Earth as we face the future. The mysteries revealed by ecology challenge us to explore afresh our habitat and to discover whether they, in fact, help us to understand the mysteries found hidden in the Bible, our traditions, our environment, and our personal worlds.

Step 4
Explore where I, through personal experience, have met the sacred in the mysteries of nature.

My high point is the exploration and celebration of mysteries I have experienced. Reflecting on my life's journey, I wonder just where and how I began to bond with Earth or domains of Earth in a personal spiritual way. Where did I begin to sense mystery as a spiritual dimension of the cosmos?

Over the centuries, people have sought to come to terms with the meaning of life and the mystery of existence in a myriad of ways. Some, including the indigenous peoples of our planet, discern their spiritual relationship with nature as part of the mystery and meaning of life. My task here is to explore afresh, in the context of our current environment, the mysteries of life that relate to our habitat, our home, and our planet, and that have spiritual overtones or undercurrents.

To do this, I will tell of my spiritual connections with creation, personal experiences of the sacred, and close encounters with mystery in nature. Each of these moments may not stand alone, but be related to a biblical text with which I resonate, and/or to a natural phenomenon revealed as a mystery through ecology. I will sometimes articulate these experiences in poetic form, to capture the depth and drama of the moment, and the mystery.

I also read the book of nature to discover the mysteries inscribed across the face of the cosmos, and the sacred written on the pages of the landscape. In this I am following the lead of Aboriginal mentors who read the landscape and identify the sacred sites, forces, stories, and song-lines that flow through their natural surroundings.

The following reflection may indicate something of my current orientation to nature and to the mysteries that impinge on my consciousness.

My World of Mystery

When I am home with Earth,
I am aware of two deep spiritual forces:
initiating impulse
and permeating presence.

I am always discovering new impulses
in Earth,
spawned by deep initiating impulses.
Impulses
to evolve and to explore,
to dance and to dine,
to mate and to nurture,
to commune and connect,
to celebrate and to empathise.

Quite simply
I am surrounded by mysteries;
amazing impulses
to be
in a billion blossoming ways.

I am also aware of
continuous expressions of a deep permeating Presence:

the presence
of alluring heights and horizons,
sacred sites and ecosystems,
silent mystery in hidden habitats,
the soul of Earth revealed in stillness.

When I am home with Earth,
I am acutely aware
Earth is there,
mystery is moving me
and Presence is present.

Step 5
Discern the wisdom needed to sustain mystery and the sacred in nature.

My aim is to stimulate new ways of experiencing and sustaining mystery as an integral part of our daily existence in this precious living habitat called Earth.

One way of promoting new spiritual awareness is through new forms of worship. The appendices to this volume include ideas for workshops and rites that bring a new sense of the sacred to those who love nature. The worship materials found on *The Season of Creation* website may be adapted to facilitate worship with nature (rather than simply expressing thanks for creation). These liturgies may also be appropriated for worship in the wild, where participants sense the spiritual in their surroundings and feel the pulses of our living planet (see www.seasonofcreation.com.au).

Another way of sustaining mystery and connecting with the spiritual will be through reading the landscape. I will place myself – and invite you to join me – in a particular landscape of our planet. In that location I shall read the landscape, sense mystery in nature, feel pulses of our planet, and meet the sacred in my environment. I will share my readings and invite you to read the same text of nature from your spiritual perspective. I will read through the eyes of my new ecological consciousness, my biblical background, and a revived spiritual awareness.

At first blush it may seem that my approach to reading nature and hearing her voice is implausible. We are aware, of course, that palaeontologists read fossil sediments from a former seabed and discover the origins of life from the Cambrian period where primal creatures with five eyes could read their underworld habitat. Geologists read layers of rocks half a million years old and identify the various eras of evolution and catastrophe on the planet. Biologists read the leaves of plants and the rings of tree trunks to discern the processes involved in flora life forms, from simple cells to massive myrtles. Ecologists now go a step further and seek to discern the communication between all these interconnected domains and life forms of our planet. I likewise seek to read nature with eyes and ears that try to discern the mysteries imbedded in all these realms of our ever-changing cosmos.

However, knowing what we know about the ecological crisis, we cannot simply explore and celebrate the mysteries as spiritual dimensions of nature and enjoy them as sources of stimulus for our faith. We also need to commit to preserving our planet and to sustaining our spiritual connections with the mysteries inherent in the habitat we call Earth as part of our purpose in life.

My end point is to covenant to sustain a sense of mystery in our planet. How might we, given our experiences of mystery, bond with Earth in such a way as to celebrate and sustain the mysteries we discern in nature? How might we be custodians of the mysteries of this sacred planet as we read its landscape – its forest pages, its mountain texts, and its ocean images? How might we be agents of healing as we feel the pulse of a suffering Earth? How might we articulate a mission to nurture the mother who has nurtured us?

Making a covenant means bonding with another party as a faithful partner ready to share and sustain a meaningful relationship. Our partner is Earth and our relationship includes the spiritual. The One who is depicted as making such a covenant with Earth after the Flood may be viewed as a witness or potential third party to this covenant.

Ultimately, such a covenant involves a deep concern for the welfare of our partner Earth, whose health has suffered in recent years because of human abuse of the planet. We are called to activate the primal mission of humans to "serve" and "sustain" Earth (Genesis 2:15).

Chapter One

The Mystery of Presence

❧

A Red Mystery

Where can I go from your spirit,
and where can I flee from your presence?
(Psalm 139:7)

Presence

Presence is a mystery that stirs my spirit. The ocean before me presents itself to me; it has a presence that impinges deeply on my consciousness. So too do the forest, the blossoming flowers, and the bats that invade my vision in the evening.

Many things exist that may never present themselves to me. Their presences are hidden. But when a presence is revealed to my consciousness and I perceive that presence, another dimension is added. Presence is more than existence; presence evokes mystery.

I now ask whether I can sense a spiritual presence within all or some domains. We have tended to sense the spiritual dimension of presence as hidden, as under the radar of everyday experience. But is it? Can I experience the mystery of the sacred in nature present around me? Can I consciously connect with the spiritual in creation whether I can see it or not?

I invite you to join me as I explore the first mystery in a rainbow of mysteries in nature.

Presence in the Scriptures

My search for spiritual presence begins by viewing afresh some sightings of Presence in the Christian scriptures.

The first sighting I would like to examine is recorded in chapter 6 of Isaiah. The images depicted in the call of this prophet suggest a scene from *Star Trek* or some other fantasy. The whole scenario is quite bizarre.

Isaiah is worshipping in the temple when he sees God mounted on a lofty throne, his royal robes flowing throughout the temple. God is surrounded by weird mythical creatures called seraphim. Seraphim are wild snakes, each with six wings of flame. Two wings enable them to fly. Two wings cover their face, presumably so they do not see God in person. And two wings, as is appropriate for modest celestial beings, cover their feet, or in less euphemistic language, their genitals.

The seraphim fly around the temple singing a famous chorus we associate with the *Sanctus*: "Holy, holy, holy in the Lord Almighty, the whole Earth is full of his glory." When Isaiah is struck dumb with a sense of uncleanness before this God, one of the seraphim touches his lips with a burning coal. Isaiah is then ready, mouth scorched and purified, to preach great oracles of doom involving impending fires of judgment.

Time and again I have sung the *Sanctus* of the seraphim in church and heard it as a traditional expression of praise (although this wild sighting of God's presence is not an experience with which I can identify).Then one day, I realised just how extraordinarily radical that text is.

The word translated "glory" *(kabod)* is a technical term for the visible presence of God. That visible Presence is often described as a cloud filled with red consuming fire. The first sighting of this fire cloud is in the wilderness prior to the events at Mount Sinai (Exodus 16:10). The murmuring of Israel provokes the appearance of God's presence in the wilderness in advance of an avalanche of quails that cover the camp.

Later, this intense fire cloud is sighted landing on Mount Sinai and covering it for six days. On the seventh day, from out of the cloud which is burning like a "devouring fire" on top of the mountain, God calls to Moses. Then Moses goes up the mountain and is enveloped in that shimmering expression of divine presence for forty days (Exodus 24:15–18).

Subsequently, God commissions Moses to build a tabernacle, a mobile sanctuary, to lead the Israelites across the wilderness. After the tabernacle is constructed, the fire cloud "fills" the tabernacle (Exodus 24:34–38). This sighting of God's presence is quite distinctive. The actual fire or Presence is located *inside* the holy sanctuary of the tabernacle, while the cloud rests above the tabernacle and leads the way for the people of God crossing the wilderness.

Later, when King Solomon constructs the temple in Jerusalem, that very same fire cloud of divine presence is said to "fill" the holy of holies in the temple (1 Kings 8:10–11). Solomon depicts this localised presence as a special privilege since the highest heaven cannot contain his deity (1 Kings 8:27). The intensity of the fire cloud that fills the temple is so great that the priests cannot serve before it.

Although these spectacular sightings of divine fire cloud do not resonate with me (they belong to the faith of an ancient tradition), I am intrigued by the cries of the seraphim. They announce that the visible presence of God "fills" Earth. And that announcement is amazingly radical, a mystery worth exploring. The visible Presence, which was once thought to fill the holy of holies, is said to fill the entire planet! Does that mean that, in some sense, our planet is a sanctuary filled with a radiant divine presence? Is our planet like a holy of holies in the cosmos? Is our planet permeated with the spiritual, alive with holiness? That is a mystery worth exploring.

One may, of course, ignore the voices of the seraphim and view the call of Isaiah as a dramatic prophetic call in which a man is summoned into the service of God through an extraordinary sighting of God's presence. It is not Isaiah's call experience, however, that resonates with me. It is, rather, the bold and radical claim that "Presence" permeates the planet. The chorus may have been sung by mythical figures called seraphim, but the text has been handed down in a meaningful prophetic tradition that remembers something of this amazing mystery.

So I ask, is this radical cry just a weird one-off angelic chorus, or can I too experience Presence throughout my planet? Can I sense Presence filling Earth, or is this chorus but another tired expression of an ancient faith? Can I reso-nate not only with a tantalising text, but also with spiritual dimensions of nature that can be designated "Presence"?

Another text that strikes a chord with me is the story of Moses near Sinai. God promises that God's presence will always go with Moses because he has found favour in the sight of God. Moses responds by reminding God that he now knows God's name, but wishes to make one final personal request to be reassured of God's support. "Please show me your glory, your presence!" Moses wants a private viewing, a special sighting. God replies that granting such a request is not possible. Moses cannot see God's face, that is, God's immediate presence. However, if Moses hides in a cleft of the rock, Presence will pass by. God will prevent Moses seeing the very face of God, but when God has passed by Moses will be able to discern, with a touch of humour, the backside of God, Presence from behind (Exodus 33:17–23).

This passage suggests that Presence is not only in the forms of a distinct ball of fire or shimmering glow on the sand that can be seen as separate entities. Presence is sensed from a distance rather than seen face to face. Presence is veiled, but still there somehow. Or, in the metaphor of this text, we sense the backside of God in creation; we do not see the face in all its flame. In this passage, Presence permeates, rather than intervenes in, creation.

By now I am bold enough to follow the lead of Moses and ask whether I too can discern the presence of God as a "face" in nature. Or have I, perhaps, experienced Presence without recognising it? Has my consciousness been aware of this spiritual dimension to Earth, a domain "filled with Presence," but not named it as such? Have I been hindered from discovering Presence by the teachings and context of my tradition?

Can I experience Presence as something other than a dramatic sighting? Can I explore the mystery of Presence experientially? God's presence as red fire is not part of my reality but can I follow the lead of some of the psalmists and hear the skies announcing the presence of God in the cosmos? (Psalm 19:1)

Presence in my tradition

My aspiration is to discover Presence in nature, to sense the sacred in creation, to resonate with the radical cry of the seraphim that Presence fills the planet. In my tradition, however, the presence of God was usually located in a heaven above rather than filling planet Earth below. As a child I would kneel at my bedside and imagine this old Father in heaven looking down on me and frowning or smiling depending on my attitude. The local scrub and the muddy swamps in our neighbourhood were not places of Presence.

When I was being confirmed, the pastor taught us three major truths about God. "God," he intoned, "is omnipotent, omniscient, and omnipresent." As the omnipotent One, God was like a Ruler on high who could create or destroy at will. As the omniscient One, God was like Father Christmas, watching our every move. God knew whether we had been bad or good, anywhere, anytime, or any place.

The image of an omnipresent One, however, presented something of a dilemma. How could the God of heaven be everywhere? How could the presence of this singular divine being called Father Almighty be located both above and below, up there and down here? The dilemma was ostensibly resolved by announcing that the presence of God was everywhere spiritually but not physically. Spiritually, God was omnipresent. Physically, God was omni-absent. Or at least that is the way it appeared to me as a youth.

Our parish preacher, in addition, cited texts like Isaiah 66:1 to justify the prevalent theology. According to that passage, God is enthroned in heaven with Earth below reduced to the category of a footstool. Earth as a footstool! The perception was that God is a discrete being intervening from above, rather than a presence vibrating through the physical world. This text does not seem consistent with the radical message of the seraphim. Or did I get it wrong, thinking the seraphim were proclaiming Presence filling the planet?

I began to wonder whether this division of reality into spiritual and physical might be a mark of theological convenience. Is Presence perhaps everywhere, permeating the entire cosmos? What if we were able to transform such memories of a distant – albeit loving – deity and connect with God's presence in creation here and now? What if the cosmology of a divided universe with God above and mortals below was not the only option true to our tradition and the Bible? What if we were to accept an invitation to discover the spiritual in creation, Presence permeating our planet, a deep divine dimension behind every inch of Earth (and the cosmos)? What if, with Isaiah, we experienced God as Presence "filling" our planet? How might that presence be sensed, experienced, discerned? Can I discern presence when I read the landscapes of Earth, or feel her pulses?

Another factor that hindered any exploration of Presence in creation in my tradition was the overwhelming impression that the physical world was quite secondary to salvation. God's presence was revealed at pivotal points in the history of salvation, from God's divine intervention at the

Exodus to the ultimate intervention in the person of Jesus Christ. These Godly interventions were part of a divine plan to bring all people to faith, especially in Jesus Christ. And it was in Jesus, the Incarnate Word of God, that we saw God's glory or presence (John 1:14). To look for Presence beyond the person of Jesus was considered a waste of time.

There was also talk about Presence in church. All three persons – God the Father, Son, and Holy Spirit – were somehow present in worship. Unfortunately, there were no sightings in my church, no explicit experiences of Presence in my pew. Presence was understood to be present (but hidden) in rites, symbols, and sermons – especially in the Word in the sermon. There was even talk of a real presence in, with, and under the bread and wine of Holy Communion. But that too was a presence we accepted by faith not by personal experience.

The church was the prime sanctuary of God's presence. The suggestion that we might experience Presence in nature was dismissed as a view akin to nature worship, or the privileged domain of forgotten mystics. No one bothered to explore the suggestion of Luther that creation was in fact *larvae Dei,* the mask of God. Exploring his insight beyond the stained glass windows of the church may have made us more aware of Presence in nature.

I vividly remember playing Satan in the play *J.B.* by Archibald MacLeish. God and Satan are depicted as two distant figures in dialogue in the heavenly council. They are looking down on Job and his family, and Satan challenges God's proud claim that Job is a model citizen. God bets

Satan that Job will stay faithful no matter what God hurls at him, and proceeds to damage Earth through many natural disasters. As Satan, I felt perfectly justified in denouncing a God who was willing to sacrifice nature for the sake of his pride. That portrait of God was not one with which I could identify, and, as it turns out, neither could Job.

This distant demanding God, for all the testimony to divine compassion, was not a presence I experienced in the natural world until I chose to take the radical chorus of the seraphim seriously.

Presence in nature

Thomas Berry regrets how, in the past, scientists have created a type of knowledge that no longer leads "to an intimate presence within a meaningful universe." The various phenomena of nature are no longer viewed as "spirit presences." Our world of meaning, he argues, is now determined through photographic and televised presentations rather than direct contact with our natural surroundings. "Our children no longer learn how to read the great Book of Nature" (1999, 15).

The worldview that has been revealed through ecology, however, invites us to return to our natural surroundings and read that great Book of Nature anew. And the mystery of Presence need no longer be elusive or inaccessible. The spiritual is as much a part of our interconnected cosmos as gravity or light.

I began my exploration of this mystery by sitting each night at a distance from a tall eucalyptus tree. It presented itself to me, a stark black image against the light grey sky at dusk. A bat might weave its way around the top. A moth might flutter around, and a parakeet might search for nectar, but the tree stood still against the sky, a gift of sheer grace. I sensed I was an integral part of the ecosystems around me.

The presence of the tree, however, became a moment in time reaching infinitely into the past and infinitely into the future. And I was privileged to be there, to sense that. Beyond the tree was an infinite world of astral presences. Within and beneath the tree was an infinite world of elements, atoms, and genes, a world revealed to me by science. Between those two worlds was the mystery of the moment, the presence of one tall tree before me.

The tree exists. Planet Earth exists. Humans exist. And that is the grace of sheer existence. Earth exists as an amazing moment in the time-space explosions of the cosmos. That is grace! But richer than existence is Presence. For the moment the tree presents itself to me, it confronts me with the mystery of Presence, a presence that permeates the planet.

Beyond the tree, the sun is setting and patterns of vivid red transform the sky into a vast galaxy of colour. The fire in the sky is not only a magnificent sight; it is also another mystery: the intricate interaction of light, atmosphere, and space coming together in what we call a sunset. As I behold the presence of the sunset before me, I resonate with the voice of the Psalmist:

The skies keep announcing the presence of El,
    And the firmament proclaims the work of God's
hands (Psalm 19:1).

A scientist may well offer a technical explanation for this phenomenon, but for me its presence is also spiritual, connecting me with the fire of El, the Creator spirit known not only to Israel, but also to the indigenous people of Canaan. The red in the sky has long been experienced as a presence that reaches beyond the sun, the sky, and the fire of the moment. The red captures the mystery of the moment.

In short, the sunset is a spiritual encounter with a mystery of creation, a mystery that may be experienced as Presence. If we return to the song of the Psalmist, we recognise that the mystery being announced by the skies is Presence filling creation. And that mystery is further described by the Psalmist as a celestial antiphon of voices echoing back and forth in creation, voices we humans may not hear but which acclaim Presence to and through all creation. Or, as the Psalmist continues,

Day speaks about it with day
And night passes on knowledge to night.
No utterance at all, no speech,
No sound can anyone hear;
Yet their voice goes out through all of Earth,
And their message to the ends of the world
(Psalm 19:2–4).

Thomas Berry's words in the Introduction about a single integral community of the Earth (1999, 4) inform this Psalm. Earth is a community of interacting presences, each presence spontaneously declaring itself to other presences and all interconnected by a deep permeating Presence. Earth is indeed filled with mystery. Presence is indeed present.

Presence in my world

All of the preceding encounters with a sense of presence barely prepared me for the day I experienced what I have come to call sacred Presence. Let me describe it in poetic language.

Suspended in Stillness

I sat in a crevice of nature, a cove on Kangaroo Island.
It was October 3, 2009. All was still; shimmering still.
No wind or wave stirred the eerie hush,
yet there was a feeling of Presence, intense, close.
It was as if nature had ceased all movement
so that I might feel her pulse.
Sounds hovered in the distance.
Then the sound of silence,
of sheer stillness,
and I was suspended
in Presence.

Is this the moment Elijah knew in that cave on God's mountain? According to the storyteller, Elijah was expecting God to pass by (just like Moses thought when he was hiding in a cleft of the rock). A great wind began to break rocks off the mountain, but God was not in the wind. After the wind, an earthquake shook the mountain. But God was not in the earthquake. Then there was a raging fire, but God was not in the fire. Finally there was stillness, sheer silence. In that stillness, Elijah experienced God's presence and heard God's voice. "Why are you here?" (1 Kings 19:11–13)

Like Elijah, I too became aware of all those loud crashes of nature with which people associate God's intervention. At the very moment I was listening in stillness, I knew of an earthquake that was rocking Sumatra and a monsoon that was smashing Pacific islands. As I listened in silence I heard voices from across the sea – the wailing of women on a beach hit by a tsunami, the cries of children whose house had been smashed by a hurricane. Was God in the storm, in the earthquake, in the tsunami? I could hear the islanders crying, "Why? Why, God, why?"

Where is God, my God? I wondered as I sat suspended in stillness, in Presence. In the monsoon? In the tsunami? In the earthquake? Or here in the stillness?

Is God above it all directing the weather from a distance? Is God silently planning the end of time when all will be still and peaceful? Or is God somewhere deep within, a part of it all, one with the drama, swirling in the seas?

The soft stillness hovered, gentle, inviting. My inner ear heard another voice in the stillness. "Can you sense my presence echoing across the ocean, penetrating the planet? Can you feel my touch as the plates of the planet grate and shudder? Can you hear my voice in the Earth? Can you see my presence in every wild wind? Can you feel the pulse of my presence in the stillness?

Then I wondered whether this stillness was revealing something more, such as the primal Presence that preceded the Big Bang. Am I suspended in a primal stillness like that mysterious moment before the big beginning? Am I in the sacred stillness of the beginning?

From within that primal stillness, I sensed an impulse from the past – an impulse to move, to evolve, to explode, to create. Then there came an endless line of impulses, interconnecting through time, crashing through the cosmos and reaching me! An endless line of explosions and quakes, births and breathing! Was this the primal pulse of creation still beating, Presence within the primal stillness?

And is that pulse, the Presence I sensed, felt in everything from earthquakes to evening breezes, from tsunamis to tears, from monsoons to trees in blossom?

I do not expect that my experience of Presence in stillness will necessarily be interpreted by others, as I have done, in the light of Elijah's moment. Nor do I expect that my resonance with the sacred in nature will be read as spiritual by all who reflect on what has been written here. It needs to be noted, however, that my experience is as much a reflection informed by ecology as by my faith background. This mystery is more than a revival of my childhood connection with nature. This mystery is a fresh spiritual understanding that comes from my connections with ecology, biblical moments, and personal experiences.

This mystery is for me the Presence that permeates all interconnected dimensions in nature, a spiritual presence that can be sensed in sheer stillness, in the domains of this planet, or in the infinite realms of the cosmos.

The mystery of Presence challenges me to reconsider the very nature of God. I can no longer resonate with an omnipotent ruler outside of the cosmos who intervenes as necessary. Nor can I accept those past doctrines that separate God from nature. My starting point is now the cry of the seraphim that the presence of God fills planet Earth. I now understand their words to mean, "The Presence which is God fills the cosmos and is revealed before our very eyes through this planet." God is that sacred Presence that permeates creation and is revealed through nature.

Sustaining the mystery of Presence

If Earth is indeed a sanctuary filled with Presence, then we are called to do more than explore the mystery of Presence or worship in that presence. We are also called to keep Earth sacred and holy. We are called to name the pollution of our planet as desecration. We are called to be priests and priestesses who serve, celebrate, and sanctify this planet. We are called to announce the mystery of Presence throughout Earth.

The Covenant

In more concrete terms, that means accepting the invitation to covenant with Earth and work with Earth as a partner in her preservation. The first commitment in such a covenant might be articulated as follows.

> *Given the mystery that planet Earth is a sanctuary filled with Presence (Isaiah 6:3), we are invited to sense Presence wherever we wander or worship on this planet, to respect Earth as sacred, and to prevent her from being desecrated.*

A public declaration of that intention could take a number of forms in either worship or social contexts. The first rite appended to this volume offers an example of a worship option. Another option could involve a public statement of identity attached to where we worship, work, or gather.

> This building is a sanctuary
> erected on the land of (*the Kaurna people*),
> located in the sanctuary called Earth,
> and thus filled with God's presence.
> Please keep God's sacred planet free from pollution.

Another way of sustaining the mystery of Presence is to find a time and place to absorb Presence. For example, I often sit high on a hill with the landscape before me, the text of nature in my sight, the songs of the planet in my ears. I sit waiting for the sunset, ready to read what I can with the eyes of my consciousness, ready to experience Presence.

The horizon is present to me. It meets the ocean in the distance. The shoreline and the trees present themselves. The clouds begin to capture the red of the sun over the horizon. The colours of the sunset change slowly from yellow, to orange, to vibrant red.

The mystery of the sunset confronts me. The whole landscape deepens into dusk. I sense in my consciousness Presence permeating all of nature before me. As I watch, I remember the words of Bruce Sanguin.

> The mystery inherent in the sunset is not a problem to be solved. It's about the feelings evoked by the beauty of the colours; it's the awareness that what we are witnessing is the slow turning of the earth away from the sun, and that our bodies and minds are preparing to enter another dimension of consciousness, deep sleep; it's the awareness that we are travelling through deep space in a sacred dance with the orb of light and heat which is responsible for our capacity to even consciously enjoy the sunset... Mystery then is the depth dimension of life, which lies beyond rational explanation (2007, 73).

Soon all is still and I am suspended in stillness. The text of nature before me reveals Presence. The sounds of nature around me celebrate Presence. And, as I read, feel, and hear, I am struck with awe. Presence has emerged as a red mystery beyond the sunset. In my own way I am sustaining the mystery of Presence as I invite you to discern Presence where you live.

And may I add a postscript to enhance the mystery. Just as the light of Venus enters the afterglow of the sunset, a bat flies through the trees. I hear her wings. The bat, despite being blind to the red sky, senses the mystery of the moment, the time to rise and fly into the sunset. The bat and I celebrate the same sunset.

Conclusion

If I dare to summarise the mystery of Presence as I have encountered it in my consciousness, I could speak of three dimensions of Presence – natural presence, permeating presence, and sacred presence.

I encounter natural presence whenever I pause in nature and let what is there before me present itself to me. Every individual thing that exists exhibits its presence if I am but aware.

Permeating presence comes to consciousness when I experience the domains in Earth interacting intensely all around me and beyond. Permeating presence integrates all other presences at any given time and place.

Sacred presence reaches me in the stillness when all other presences are, as it were, suspended and another dimension surfaces. Sacred presence hovers for me in moments of deep silence.

I believe, however, that because of my past conditioning, I have failed to discern the most extraordinary dimension – that of sacred presence. The sacred I have always understood as hidden – either deep within me, or in nature, or in a sacrament. A sacred presence, then, even if it permeates the planet, remains unseen. But does it? Why should it?

In the light of this exploration and these experiences, I now believe that the sacred presence, the Presence one may call God, is not hidden. When I see the presences of trees, hills, oceans, and skies before me, they are the revelation of Presence before my very eyes. That Presence not only fills Earth as some sort of hidden force, but it surfaces in the very presences we see before us.

If a glass is "filled" with rich red wine, I smell, taste, and behold its presence. The same is true of Presence in this planet – especially at sunset. Behold and sense the Presence called God!

Blessing

May the radiant Presence
filling this sanctuary called Earth
help us discover a holy of holies
shimmering red among the trees
in a location we love.

Chapter Two

The Mystery of Being Earth-Born

An Orange Mystery

*Naked I came from my mother's womb
and naked I shall return there. (Job 1:21)*

Being an Earth being

I am not only a human being, I am also an Earth being, one among millions of other Earth beings, past and present and future.

And I am composed of the same matter that makes this planet what it is – both earth and Earth. I am an Earth child, born of Earth and made of earth.

I am made of the very orange clay that permeates this planet. Or as Macy says,

> Matter is made of rock and soil. It too is pulled by the magma that circulates through our planet heart and roots such molecules into biology. Earth pours through us, replacing each cell in the body every 7 years...we ingest and excrete Earth, are made from Earth. I am that. You are that (Macy, 1996, 501).

I belong to a fragile web of interconnected and interdependent fragments and forces on this planet. And the matter that emanated from primordial times in the cosmos evolved into conscious Earth beings, who reflect the spiritual imbedded in the material. Matter and spirit are not separate.

Earth beings in the Scriptures

We are introduced to the mystery of being earth creatures made of orange clay in the challenging creation myth of Genesis 2. The narrator makes it clear that the narrative is not part of recent history, but set in the primordial time when YHWH brought Earth and the skies into being. The setting is "in the beginning," a barren world before any life forms except God existed, and one quite different from that depicted in Genesis 1. (A more technical analysis of Genesis 2 is found in my *Earth Bible Commentary* [Habel 2011, chapter 3].)

The primal world is described explicitly as having "no plant of the field," "no rain," and "no one to care for the ground (*adamah*)." And because there is no one to care for *adamah*, the first creature made from *adamah* is Adam.

The explicit reason for making Adam is further clarified in Genesis 2:15, where it becomes apparent that Adam was formed in order to "serve" and "keep" *adamah*. In other words, the first Earth being is created for the benefit of Earth, not vice versa.

The intimate relationship between Adam and *adamah*, however, is not due only to the purpose of Adam. Adam is also made from the very stuff of *adamah*, the orange or red soil of the fertile ground. *Adamah* is both the source of Adam and the reason for Adam's existence.

Adam is an Earth being, like each of us, created from *adamah* to "serve" and "preserve" the forest of Eden, and by implication the ground/Earth which is the source of all life. The act of preserving indicates a dimension of care that goes beyond simply working or serving in the forest. Preserving, or keeping the forest is a primordial task. Adam is *adamah's* keeper! The call for humans to preserve old-growth forests in our current environmental context echoes the primordial mission of Adam.

The creation of Adam is depicted as the work of an artisan or potter taking some soil from *adamah* and moulding it into a human form. The animation of this human form happens when the divine artisan breathes life into the nostrils. The breath or air from God that the first human receives is the same as that which all living creatures breathe (Genesis 7:22). As a result of this breath, each creature is a living Earth being. There is no indication that humans have a soul or inner-being that differentiates them from other Earth beings. The same spirit or breath of God animates all life.

This orange mystery is that all living beings are Earth beings made of clay and animated with air or, in spiritual terms, the atmosphere, which is identified as the breath of God. Orange is the colour of the clay, the ground of being for all Earth beings.

After the so-called fall in Genesis 3, Earth welcomes all Earth beings home when they die and return to clay. Or as Job says, in the opening response to his personal crisis, "naked I came from my mother's womb and naked I shall return there" (Job 1:21). Job acknowledges that he is an Earth being, that Earth is his mother, and that his mother receives him again in death.

These texts celebrate the mystery that humans, like all other creatures, are intricate Earth beings animated by the breath of

God. One of the Psalmists, however, goes a step further and celebrates the spiritual dimension of our origins in Earth.

As we begin reading Psalm 39, the Psalmist seems to play a trick. The Psalmist appears to be describing the wondrous process of God creating a delicate piece of artwork deep inside the Psalmist's human mother. God is praised for the amazing way in which the human frame is knitted together to form a magnificent embryo. All of this brilliant crafts-manship is undertaken by God in secret.

Surprisingly, at the end of that section of the poem we discover that the womb is actually Mother Earth. The Psalmist announces that he was "intricately woven in the depths of Earth." The poem might be expressed as follows.

Let me sing of my birth
my beginnings as an Earth being.
I have sensed deep within me a mystery,
how the fingers of God
moulded all my inner parts
knitting together the web of my inner being
deep in my mother's womb.
God kept every feature of my frame in sight
deep in secret below.
God wove together my body
in the depths of Earth, mother Earth.
What a wonder
to be Earth born!
(Psalm 139:13-15)

In Genesis 1 we encounter another birth narrative – the birth of Earth! (Genesis 1:1–13) In the past, most scholars have interpreted this text as God bringing order out of chaos. A close reading of it, however, reveals Earth waiting in the waters, like an embryo in a primal womb ready to be born but as yet unformed. God, meanwhile, hovers above the waters like a midwife (Habel, 2011, chapter 2).

God then creates light so that Earth can be seen when she is born, and space in the skies above where Earth can appear. On the third day we enjoy the birth. God does not say, "Let there be Earth," but rather, "Let the waters separate/burst so that the land may appear." The land appears and God names the new baby Earth. God brings the baby to life by causing vegetation to emerge. Finally, God looks at baby Earth and says, "Very good" or "Wonder-full."

The opening myth of Genesis is not simply about the creation of the natural world. It also tells of God relating to this world as something wonderful, a child to be loved. If Earth were to tell her story in her own words, it might go something like this.

I am Earth, Baby Earth

In the beginning, I was waiting deep in the primal waters, the primal womb. I was waiting in the darkness like an embryo waiting to be born. Above, God hovered over the waters, like a midwife.

Then God said, "Light. We need some light so that Earth can been seen." And light entered the primal darkness.

Then God said, "Space. We need some space for Earth to appear." So God placed a canopy over the waters with space below it.

Light! Space! Action!
Then God said, "Let the primal waters part and let the land waiting beneath appear." Suddenly the waters burst and I came forth, a newborn child of God.

Do you know what God named me? Earth!
Yes, I am Baby Earth.
To demonstrate that I was alive and breathing, God said, "Let Earth bring forth vegetation, every kind of flora." Soon I was really alive and green!

God looked at me, this new living being, this baby from the deep, and said, "Beautiful!"

These Scripture texts illustrate that there were ancient biblical traditions that recognised the mystery of birth both in the origin of Earth and in the emergence of Earth beings. Both Earth and Earth beings were viewed as having a spiritual dimension, an intimate connection with a God who birthed Earth from the primordial deep, and Earth beings from within Earth's womb.

Being an Earth being in my tradition

In my experience, the Christian tradition downplayed and devalued the intimate connection of humans with Earth. The Earth dimension of my being was but matter, transitory, and frail – dust destined to return to dust.

Into this transitory piece of matter, I was told, God infused a spiritual core, a soul or spirit. (When and how God did this was never explained satisfactorily to me.) This spiritual core was understood to be eternal, that true inner me destined – if all went well – to a life with God in heaven. I was part temporal and part eternal, body and soul.

The problem I faced in my tradition was the belief that birth into the world was not clean. Not only were women, after giving birth, obliged to undergo a purification rite in church before they could attend Holy Communion, but the baby itself carried with it a hereditary element called sin, or more specifically, original sin.

This impediment was removed through the sacrament of Baptism. The water of baptism washes the baby clean and baby is "born" a second time. However, the full import of what this ritual meant for me became apparent after the following experience.

The baby cried a little, the celebrant proceeded with the rite of passage, and I smiled knowingly. I had heard the script of the Baptism ritual a hundred times before – the commission of Christ, the admonition to the godparents, and the welcome into God's family. Suddenly, at age seventy, I heard a line from the liturgy as if for the first time: "You are being adopted into the family of God."

Adopted! The words echoed in my mind. I was adopted, adopted into the church, into the family of God. God was my Father, my adoptive Father. Through baptism I was "born of water and the spirit." So, my family was now a spiritual family, a spiritual home. I emerged from the waters of baptism as a child from its spiritual mother's womb and was "born again." In the language of the sacrament, my adoption was official in the eyes of the community. I was God's child and my new family name was "Christian." I was, in the words of a well-known hymn, "a child and heir of heaven." I was no longer an Earth being.

Yes, I was adopted. But for the first time in my life I wondered, Who are my "biological" parents? From whom was I separated or removed in order to be adopted into this spiritual family? Who are my "birth parents"? Who? Not my human father and mother. They were also part of the family of God. From whom then was I separated? From whom was I taken, stolen, or rescued?

I felt rather guilty asking this question. After all, I was also a celebrant who had often performed Baptism, the "rite of adoption." I should know! The urge to discover my lost parent or parents, however, compelled me to begin a new search. I began a journey that took me back to the texts of the Bible I thought I knew so well.

If the God of the church is my adoptive parent, my spiritual father, who is my original parent, my biological parent? Strange as it may seem, my studies in ecology began to make sense; they became more than academic exercises. They provided a personal perspective on my origins.

Is my biological parent Earth? Why not? Every part of me comes from Earth – the air, fire, water, minerals, and micro-organisms that my body comprises are all from Earth. They belong to an endless cycle of interconnected Earth components that have hung together in ever-changing patterns in my body for seventy years. I am an Earth-child, a dimension of my existence that I now need to explore and understand. Earth, it would seem, is my biological parent. I am an Earth being, not just a human being.

Nothing was ever said to me over the years about my biological parent. Earth was not publicly declared to be an unfit parent – or even a parent. In fact, Earth was conspicuous by her absence. Those who related to Earth spiritually were denounced as animists or worse. The church taught that as a human child, I was "conceived and born in sin" and therefore damned by God. My baptism and adoption rescued me from that verdict and incorporated me into a life-giving family. I was saved from my sinful biological origins. But what did that mean? Had I been rescued from Earth?

The belief of my church community that I was a sinful human child in need of rescue, in spite of my condition as an innocent newborn, was based primarily on a story in Genesis 3 and Saint Paul's interpretation of that story in his letters to the Romans and Galatians. The so-called original sin of Adam and Eve was viewed as a primal force that rendered all babies corrupt by nature. I was born a corrupt Earth baby! Some members of my faith community argued that Earth was also corrupt as a result of the apparent fall of this primal couple into sin. A fallen creation accompanied a fallen humanity.

My church tradition largely ignored the reality that we are Earth beings, like other Earth beings, and focused on the belief that we, as human beings with souls, were superior and different from all other creatures. We were also told that some sciences, like psychology, verified this. Our kinship with the rest of nature was also countered by the doctrine of the *imago Dei*. This doctrine not only raises human status above other Earth creatures but also provides a mandate to dominate non-human Earth beings and subdue Mother Earth. Listen to the text:

So God made humans *(adam)* in his own image,
In the image of God, he made them;
male and female he created them.
Then God blessed them and said to them:
"Be fruitful and multiply; fill Earth and subdue it;
have dominion over the fish of the sea, over the
    birds of the air
and over every living thing that moves on Earth"
(Genesis 1:27–28).

In spite of some efforts to soften this text, the verbs for have dominion/rule (*rada*) and subdue/crush (*kabash*) are harsh and overpowering. And this text has been used to justify human efforts to harness nature, exploit creation, and bring Earth under human control (Habel 2011, chapter 2).

In my Christian tradition I now identify a range of texts, teachings, and attitudes that reduce Earth to a disposable body of matter. They also imply that Earth was created for humans to inhabit, tame, and harness while en route to heaven. The option that Earth is the true mother of humans – body, mind, and consciousness – was rejected as a residue of pagan thought.

Being an Earth being in nature

After years of being conditioned to think of ourselves as superior beings, it is not that easy to come home to Earth and identify ourselves as Earth beings. Recent findings of ecology can help us. We belong, after all, to a fragile web of interconnected and interdependent forces on this planet.

The common origin of all life, including humans, is now widely recognised by biologists and ecologists. Humans are "born of Earth," as David Suzuki and others write. The earth, air, fire, and water that have long been viewed as the elements of creation are all necessary for humans (and indeed the whole planet) to exist. As David Suzuki and Kathy Vanderlinden write,

Air, water, earth, and fire – these are the substances that support all life. Together with the sum total of that life, they maintain the planet, keep it fit for life. As we explore each element in turn, looking at its origins, its function on the planet and our intimate relationship with it, we will begin to understand our indissoluble connection with the centre. We are creatures of the Earth, and everything we learn about the Earth teaches us about ourselves (Suzuki, 1999, 38).

As Lloyd Geering points out, there is, however, a latent consistency between the myth about the creation of Adam and the findings of ecology. We are indeed formed of the dust of the ground and will return to dust in death. For as Geering says,

> The biblical proposition that we are made of Earth remains basically unchanged (in ecology), though of course we are now more sophisticated and know that the "dust" we are made of consists chiefly of atoms of carbon, hydrogen, nitrogen, and oxygen. And whereas the biblical myth pictured God forming us much as a child makes mudpies, we are now aware of the complex nature of human physiology. The lifeless atoms of which we are composed are united in the most intricate designs to form the myriad of life cells and the many internal organs that constitute the human organism (2009, 116–17).

The mystery of this human organism ought not to be ignored. In ecological terms we are Earth beings mysteriously interconnected with the soil, the environment, and the atmosphere that surrounds us (in biblical terms, the ground, the garden, and the breath from God). Or as Lloyd Geering suggests,

> The biblical myth acknowledges this new ecological insight as well. After the fashioning of the body from dust, says the Bible, God breathed his breath into it. Since Hebrew uses the same word to mean breath, spirit, wind, and air, we can translate the ancient myth into modern terminology by saying that though we humans are made of the same elements as are found in the ground beneath our feet, we come alive and stay alive only if supported by the correct atmosphere. Indeed, we cannot live more than about two minutes without breathing it (2009, 117).

While the primal myth of Genesis 2 may suggest a latent consistency with the findings of ecology, the Christian tradition I know did not discern that connection. The Earth part of our being was viewed as sinful and secondary. We saw ourselves, in the last analysis, as spiritual beings, trapped in a body but destined for heaven.

Ecology makes it clear that we are born of Earth, nurtured by Earth, and received back into Earth in death. We are Earth beings, and Earth is our Mother. Every one of us is composed of the various elements of Earth, the very matter that this planet comprises. An awareness of this ecological mystery has long been recognised by indigenous people such as the Dakota. Luther Standing Bear once said,

> Dakota children understand that they are of the soil and the soil of us, that we have the birds and beasts that grow with us, on soil. A bond exists between all things because they all drink the same water and breathe the same air (Suzuki, 1999, 52).

Birth is the mystery of endless expressions of life emerging from Earth. Earth is a massive womb from which an unlimited diversity of Earth beings are born. Humans are but one such child of Earth. And I am but one such Earth baby.

Earth too was born. Astral scientists tell us that Earth is a piece of stardust, a minute fragment of galactic matter spinning through space. Earth is but one of millions of planets that circle suns and reflect their light. Apparently Earth was born mysteriously long, long ago, somewhere in space – so the scientists say – with a big bang! I do not know precisely how my biological parent was born and matured, but I am fascinated by the way the mysterious beginnings of Earth are intuitively imagined by human beings. We have, it seems, a deep yearning to know about the origins of our parent as well as ourselves, a deep yearning that I now designate as spiritual.

My life as an Earth being

I am aware that I was separated from Earth and adopted into the family of God and that Earth was never mentioned as being my parent. I wonder, however, whether I can uncover memories of Earth as my parent.

When I was a boy on the farm, I had a genuine kinship with the land, the bush, and the creeks alive with eels. I remember my father taking me into the dry fields at the end of summer. We walked across the ground about to be prepared for sowing before the rains came and he would kneel, take a handful of soil, hold it in his palms for some time, and then let it run slowly through his fingers back to the ground. In that moment he seemed to connect with the very soul of the soil as he said, "Good earth. You are good earth." As I reflect on that experience, it seems to me my father was talking to Earth as he would a parent, though he would probably never admit to such an idea.

My brother and I felt at home in the dense scrub, wandering among the eucalypts or deep in the growing grain. In spite of Sunday sermons that directed our eyes toward heaven, we lived with our feet on the ground – even *in* the ground. I think we loved Earth, even if we never articulated our feelings.

When I speak with people in my faith community who have lived on the land – farms, vineyards, bush – they express a similar bond with the land. And that bonding, it seems to me, has biological, psychological, and spiritual dimensions. We may have been taught that God and our eternal home were in heaven, but our hearts were here on Earth with the trees, soil, and the soul of a particular location. A feeling of connection with Earth as kin still lingers in our memories – at least in mine.

The beginnings of my recent return home to Earth as an Earth being are reflected in the following poem.

My Clay Feet

The first thing I discovered
is that I have clay feet,
clay body
and clay mind.

Like all other beings on Earth
I am made of matter.
I eat, drink, and breathe the basic elements of Earth
every day of my existence.
Earth defines my identity.

Every single day,
I eat and excrete clay.
Earth pours through me,
replacing each cell in my body every seven years.
That makes me
eleven Earth years old!

I am totally
dependent
on the various elements of Earth for survival.
The matter that comprises this planet,
the oxygen in the atmosphere necessary for us to breathe,
the moisture in the clouds essential for us to enjoy a drink,
and the microbes in the soil
vital for us to receive our daily bread.

The clay of Earth
is the ground of my being.

I have the same feet of clay
as every other domain of this planet.
I am an Earth being
in search of my roots
in Earth.

The realisation that I am an Earth being and that I had
been adopted by the church meant that I now faced numerous questions, not only about my tradition, but also about
my spiritual identity. It is one thing to recognise my physical roots in nature, it is quite another to discern my sacred
connections with creation, or more specifically, with Earth.

I cannot put my finger on a moment when I was enlight-
ened by a dramatic encounter with the truth of my spiritual connection with Earth. But the more I reflected on the
mystery of birth, the more I appreciated a spiritual reality. I
always knew it was present, but it took time for that reality
to become clear.

My Earth Moment

As I reflect on my journey
I often wonder
just where it all began.
What moment sparked my desire
to find my beginnings.

After all,
I was happy in my adoptive family,
I was a leader in my community
with my name in print
and my songs in demand.
What more could I want?

In my studies of the Bible and the traditions
of my adoptive family,
I explored many approaches.
I analysed the literature,
I investigated the history,
I explored the culture.

Then ecology came onto the scene.
Just another science,
or so I thought!
Strange as it may seem,
ecology became personal.
Ecology confronted me
with a view of the world I could not ignore.
Ecology challenged my cosmology
and my faith.

Instead of being another science
that let me view nature with detachment
because I was a superior intellectual being
with a mandate to dominate creation,
ecology revealed to me who I was:
an Earth being!

An acorn sprouts, an egg hatches, a planet appears – not by choice but by virtue of a deep hidden impulse. An impulse deep within moves things to come into being, to appear, to be born. That deep impulse, from the beginning of time, has been the power leading to new things, new life, new creatures. And that impulse, working through this planet called Earth, has brought numerous Earth beings into being, of which I am one. I am because of that impulse. And I have no qualms about declaring that mysterious hidden impulse spiritual – or God, if you choose.

Sustaining the mystery of being an Earth being

When I come to the mission of sustaining the mystery of my identity as an Earth being, I begin by recalling the words of Luther, who rejoices in the belief that "God made me together with all creatures." This leads me to the conclusion that

they (non-human creatures) are our fellow creatures, and in a sense neighbours, because they like us have been created by God and formed from the soil of the earth. Our care of Earth begins by embracing our creaturely bond with Earth and its creatures. Earth suffers when we seek to be more than creatures, when we seek to be gods and rise above our physical nature (Report, 2010, 31).

I also return to the ancient tradition of Genesis 2 where the primal mission given to the first Earth creatures is to care for Earth, or in the words of verse 15, to "serve and preserve" the forest of Eden. Significantly the verb serve (*abad*) means to serve as would a priest or a labourer. Just as significant is the fact that this verb "serve" is the diametric opposite of the verb to rule (*rada*) found in the mandate to dominate in chapter one of Genesis.

An awareness of my identity as an Earth being, born of Earth, composed of Earth, and nourished by Earth, moves me to take yet another step and pursue the task of coming home to Earth to love and care for my primal parent. As I return home, I seek to explore and sustain the mystery of my identity as an Earth being.

I may locate a place where the colours of Earth can be seen, especially the colours of rock, soil, and desert sand. As I let these colours penetrate my consciousness, I become aware that I am one with Earth, that I am an Earth being. I may hold some orange clay and celebrate my journey home to be one with my mother. I may also sense my spiritual kinship with the land as my Aboriginal brothers and sisters do. And I may invoke a blessing to activate my faith as an Earth being.

The Covenant

I may also accept the invitation to covenant with Earth as my mother and to work with Earth as a partner in the preservation of this sacred planet. This invitation to bond with Earth might be articulated as follows.

> *Given the mystery that all living beings are Earth beings originating from the same orange clay of Mother Earth, we are invited to affirm our identities as Earth beings and to activate our primal mission to be partners with Earth, nurturing and preserving all life on Earth (Genesis 2:5, 15).*

Conclusion

Exploring and celebrating our connections with Earth enable us to shed the tradition that views having an Earth Mother as a pagan concept to be rejected. Earth is indeed our Mother, the very source of our being.

Returning home to Mother Earth brings us face to face with memories of Earth, and to an appreciation of Earth as a living planet where all Earth beings are nourished.

We can also affirm and celebrate other Earth beings as our kin – brothers and sisters evolving from the same elements that interact and combine to create very diverse relatives. We are all Earth-born!

Within the matter of this planet there is also mystery, that spiritual dimension that moves Earth not only to celebrate life but also to direct life in a myriad of new ways. Evolution is a sacred mystery that impinges on our consciousness as Earth beings.

In a Sacred Cave

Some years ago I helped the rainbow spirit elders of
Queensland
publish a volume entitled *Rainbow Spirit Theology*.
As we read and wrote together we listened to the land.
They taught me to listen to country,
to be kin with the land,
to be an Earth being.
Later I walked with Willie, a rainbow spirit elder,
and visited sacred caves near Cooktown
where local Aborigines were born
and their bones buried when they died.
We saw where women sat to give birth
and where they buried the afterbirth,
linking with the rainbow spirit in Earth below.
Then I saw an image of the rainbow spirit on the cave wall,
a presence without a face,
spirit stirring consciousness.
I sensed then I was indeed born of Earth,
kin with all Earth beings
and connected with the spirit of country.

Blessing

May the spirit of Earth
confirm that I am her child
and help me celebrate anew
the mystery of my origin
and all my kin in her family.

Chapter Three

The Mystery of Wonder

A Gold Mystery

*Three things are too wonderful for me,
four I do not understand. (Proverbs 30:18)*

Wonder

I wonder sometimes about wonder. Wonder is a mystery with two facets. There are objects of wonder, and there is wondering.

On the one hand, we speak of the wonders of nature – those objects, impulses, and presences that amaze and astound us. These may be as massive as the Grand Canyon and Uluru, or as minute as a delicate spider. These wonders of nature have intrinsic worth or, we might say, intrinsic wonder. They are not handy resources for humanity to abuse.

On the other hand, we react to natural phenomena with wonder and awe. There is a dimension of our consciousness that not only sees, senses, and feels what is present before us, but also reacts with wonder – what I would call the mystery of wonder.

As Val Webb says,

> Something in us wants to make sense of the world and especially our part in it. "Wonder" is a "wonder-full" word for this quest, with its double meaning of breathtaking awe and wondering about mystery (2010, viii).

In a world bursting with wonders, I invite you to explore the mystery of wonder, and the Wonder of wonders.

Note

Often the term wonder, in the Christian tradition, follows the lead of the Bible and refers to great deeds of God. We speak of signs and wonders, and mean events like God rescuing God's people from Egypt or making the sun stand still for Joshua. Such events, however, are not dimensions of nature as it manifests itself or the sacred in nature, and are not what I am referring to here when I speak of the mystery of wonder. Rather, they are extreme acts of God intervening in the course of nature, performing miraculous deeds that defy natural law, or demonstrating the power of an almighty force beyond the given eco-systems of the planet.

Wonder in the Scriptures

The mystery of intrinsic wonder and worth in the Bible is here linked with the colour (yellow) gold, which is readily associated with worth and good, with energy, and the wondrous impulses of creation. In chapter one of Genesis, God "saw" the creation and declared it "very good"; or in modern terms, "wonder-full." God beholds all of nature and declares it to have intrinsic worth by the wonder of its very existence.

However, the text that portrays the phenomenon of wonder in a bold and provocative way is Job 38, although we must recognise the satire and humour that the storyteller employs when presenting the whirling tirade of God against Job.

God confronts Job with seven wonders of the world – an ecological confrontation. Each wonder is veiled in a mystery that challenges Job's anthropocentric view of the world. God forces Job to stop focusing on his personal miseries and confront the mysteries of the universe.

We need to remember that Job is depicted as one of the wise of the ancient world and one of the greatest (Job 1:1–3). The wise in the ancient Near East were equivalent to our modern scientists. They observed nature and sought to understand its ways or laws. Job, however, had accused God of using wisdom to destroy rather than maintain nature (Job 12:13–15). Now God, as the supreme scientist, takes Job to task and confronts him with the wonders of nature.

The seven wonders of Earth

The wonder of Earth! God portrays the first wonder as a magnificent edifice called Earth, carefully designed, measured, and constructed. Job is challenged to grasp the mystery of its origins and its solid foundations. After all, says God sarcastically, you were there when I completed the edifice called Earth and you heard a grand chorus of celestial beings celebrating when the cornerstone was finally set in place.

The wonder of oceans! The second wonder is the sea that surrounds the land. With a measure of humour, this massive wonder is described as a baby that comes from the womb and is then wrapped in baby clothes and placed in a playpen. The playpen is the (land) boundary beyond which baby Sea is not permitted to crawl, precisely because God says, "No further, baby!" With this playful imagery Job is confronted by the wonder of the ocean and the mystery of waters that stay in place and do not flood the land.

The wonder of light! Another wonder is the phenomenon of light whose abode has been hidden in the darkness since the beginning of time. If Job were as old as time, declares God sarcastically, Job would have been present in the primordial to solve the mystery of light. As it is, the wonder of where light is ultimately located in the universe remains a mystery.

The wonder of stars! The stars represent a domain of wonders controlled by the laws of heaven. The mystery of how the constellations traverse time and space leaves humans, like Job, totally amazed. God challenges Job, who claims to be a wise scientist and know the world of nature, to take the laws of the skies and use them to establish order on Earth.

The wonder of weather! The advent of storms, with thunder, lightning, and rain, presents another fascinating wonder. The mystery of the origin of everything from dewdrops to hoarfrost leads us to wonder whether all these flow from mysterious sources in the sky, sources God humorously describes as the father of rain and dewdrops and the mother of ice and hoarfrost. Climate is a mystery that baffled the ancient scientist.

The wonder of the deep! The deep here confronts us with a wonder that challenges our understanding of the cosmos, the domains beneath and beyond our vision. In Job's world, the depths hide the doors of death, the gates of darkness. Beneath the ocean, the wonder of the deep is viewed as a truly terrifying mystery of the cosmos.

The wonder of clouds! The final wonder of the physical universe is the atmosphere. Clouds can produce floods of water and flashes of lightning. But the ultimate mystery is the wisdom imbedded in their being that guides them to provide the moisture needed for life on Earth. Or, asks God with another hint of humour, who tilts the bottles of heaven and causes the rain to turn dust into clods of mud?

God's challenge to Job, however, is not only to face the mysteries of these great wonders of the cosmos, but also to recognise their intrinsic worth and independence. They are not under human control or created for human benefit. They are wonders that exist as mysteries in their own right and with their own integrity.

Job's encounter with these wonders is a spiritual experience that changes his life. He declares that facing the mystery of these wonders means *seeing* God, rather than just hearing about a Creator. The sacred can be experienced in the wonders of nature. Job no longer has a reason to sit as a plaintiff in dust and ashes. He can move on and celebrate life (Job 42:1–6). In short, when Job views the wonders of nature, he claims to "see" God.

Too Wonderful!

Too wonderful!
I saw things too wonderful for words.
Caught in the eye of a whirlwind
I was summoned to behold in amazement
the primal foundations of Earth,
the depths of darkness in the underworld,
the source of rains that fall in the wilderness,
the hidden wisdom in the clouds,
the distant mystery of the constellations,
the uncontrollable wild oxen,
the soaring eagle and the odd ostrich.
All that I saw was wonderful, so very good.
In what I saw, I saw God.

Wonder in my tradition

Job's experience is a bold testimony to the spiritual dimension of wonder celebrated in some passages of the Scriptures. Sad to say, tradition often leads us to focus on other passages where the intrinsic worth and wonder of nature are not evident in the same way.

In the past, my church has rarely moved beyond saying thanks for this planet as a habitat and a resource to be exploited. The option of exploring the mystery, wonder, and intrinsic worth of every aspect of creation has been given much less attention. We have not been encouraged to experience the divine impulses at work in nature and affirm the intrinsic worth of nature. We have been ready to say that Earth is amazing, but, after all, it was created for humans to use as they see fit. Moreover, the wonder of Earth is considered relative when compared to the wonders yet to be revealed in heaven above or in the life to come.

In this context, it is also important to reconsider the doctrine of a fallen creation. Traditional theology holds that when the first humans fell from grace in the so-called Garden of Eden, their deed was so evil that all creation also fell and became corrupt. Creation was declared "very good" by the Creator when first created. Was it declared "very bad" after the fall? The ground was "cursed" to make labour difficult for Adam. But does that make creation a fallen reality? And anyway, that curse on the ground is apparently removed after the Flood (Genesis 8:21). God makes a covenant with creation after the Flood, thereby saying sorry and affirming its intrinsic worth.

Some believe that Earth is not only fallen, she is temporal, transient, and destined for disposal. Heaven, however, is permanent. God created Earth with a built-in obsolescence, so Earth is much less valuable than heaven. According to some popular preachers, Earth will continue to deteriorate until its final destruction at the hand of God. Before that day of wrath, however, the faithful will be caught up in the Rapture to escape the final conflagration.

This orientation views Earth and the entire physical universe as living out its last hours before the end. The preservation of Earth is, therefore, not a matter of paramount importance. Ecological movements merely defer the inevitable. A few nuclear blasts, holes in the ozone layer, or devastating droughts are simply portends of the denouement.

By contrast, God, the spiritual world, and heaven are changeless and eternal. And humans (and only humans) are given a core that does not die, a core that is variously called a soul or a spirit. This spiritual core is eternal, a piece of the spiritual world of God above dwelling temporarily in a decaying body here below. The body – flesh and blood – may be alive but it is not spiritual. The spiritual component is deep within, waiting for its release to be with God above. Wonder is associated with being saved by God from decay and a fallen creation, rather than seeing the mystery in nature before our very eyes.

My aim here is to shed these doctrines and affirm the reality that all of Earth is a complex of spiritual connections filled with mystery, wonder, and intrinsic worth. Doctrines that devalue Earth deserve to be filed in the wastebasket of history.

I invite you to relate to creation not as fallen but as fantastic; not as corrupt but as capable of majesty and mystery; not as mere matter but as a source of sacred wonder. Humans may have brought curses on Earth by their greed but Earth in her goodness has not cursed us.

You may also wish to reflect personally on what biblical texts or church traditions have hindered your focus on the intrinsic worth of all creation. What doctrines of the church have diminished the wonder of Earth? Has the doctrine of a fallen creation influenced your relationship with creation and hindered your desire to find spiritual connections with Earth? I have come to realise that nature is a wonder-full world that reflects God's presence, not God's curse.

Wonder in nature

It might be argued that the wonders throughout the cosmos can be explained in terms of evolution, or an evolutionary God. We might, for example, follow the lead of Bruce Sanguin, who writes:

> How, then, are we to understand an evolutionary God? This God would need to be immanent in the process of evolution, not as a controlling presence but as the cosmic urge to self-transcendence. This God would be the hidden wholeness, the non-coercive intelligence nudging hydrogen and helium molecules to organize into galaxies; galaxies to birth solar systems; and cells to cluster together in formations of increasing elegance, beauty and diversity (Sanguin, 2007, 121).

Evolution may suggest that God is the perpetual nudging of the elements to form the wonders of the cosmos. For me, however, knowing that these components are connected over space and time intensifies the mystery. Each Earth being is but a minuscule moment of matter in the process of evolution. But somehow, Earth nano-beings are connected with the cosmos, the whole of space and time. The wonder of it all is overwhelming! Perhaps then God is the "wondrous web in evolution" that connects all the wonders, whether minute or massive. If so, every connection is a spiritual wonder.

Wonder, then, is one domain where science and faith can explore mystery together. As Val Webb writes,

> Science and religion can meet for coffee today, not only over the tired old discussions about evolution, but over another word – "wonder" – which describes their joint passion. Together they can respond to the metaphorical imagery of "earth as a magic moment in the cosmos, a sacred site" (Webb, 2010, 58).

From the perspective of ecology, if we reflect on the seven wonders that confronted Job, the mystery is even more intense. The origin of Earth as a planet may be amazing, but her unique evolution into a complex living body of interrelated organisms is a mystery unknown elsewhere in our galaxy.

The oceans may cover two-thirds of this planet, yet they are like the waters of baptism that surround, sustain, and celebrate the land masses of Earth. How these waters remain in place on the planet within boundaries established by the balancing forces of gravity remains a mystery.

Light has long been a wonder that surrounds us, whether it is viewed as radiation from the sun or reflected waves arriving from distant space. The wonder of light is revealed in the presence of intense supernovas and in the mystery of photosynthesis. Our green planet is dependent on light from the sun acting in cooperation with chlorophyll.

The wonder of stars still fascinates us, whether we are scientists or songwriters. The sparkle of constellations may have taken millions of light years to reach us. Our fragile eyes connect, in an instant, with fragments of light that reach back to galaxies that emerged with the Big Bang.

With our awareness of climate change, weather poses a new mystery. Weather is interconnected not only with winds and storms, but with ocean currents, carbon dioxide levels in the air, and the rising temperature of the atmosphere. The mystery of how climate is balanced suggests another wonder we need to explore.

The wonder of the deep are domains we have yet to explore – whether it be dark matter or bright galaxies. Scientists, it is reported, have discovered a new cluster of stars 13 *billion* light years away. The deep within each molecule of matter is just as mysterious. Scientists may now be able to hear bacteria making sounds, but their language remains a mystery.

The wonder of clouds is linked to a specific mystery of nature called wisdom that we will explore in chapter 6 of this book. Clouds, like all other domains or components of nature, are not simply arbitrary patterns of moisture in the sky above us. In the biblical text of Job, clouds contain wisdom; in ecological terms the laws of nature enable clouds to float through the air and function as a source of life (water) for all Earth and Earth beings.

Whatever mysteries of evolution or ecology we may explore, we need to be conscious of more than wonder in what confronts us. Every wonder is more than a show; it is an expression of intrinsic worth and ultimately of Presence.

Every mystery is more than a challenge for scientific exploration; it has a spiritual dimension that invites us to celebrate the sacred in every wonder.

Wonder in my world

Wonder about an object of wonder can itself be something of a journey, as Keen demonstrated (1969, 88). With Keen, I believe the first stage is being "wonderstruck," amazed at what we see, surprised by a stunning reality before us. The second stage is asking why. What is this mystery, how do I understand this wonder? Finally, in the face of something that is a genuine mystery, I celebrate – perhaps even revere – the scenario and revel in what is indeed a true wonder.

Let me illustrate my experience by recalling my first encounter with Uluru, formerly known as Ayers Rock, a wonder at the sacred centre of Australia. When I first saw it I was absolutely amazed to behold such a huge and beautiful golden rock emerging from the vast flat landscape of the Outback, the red desert in central Australia. The Rock stood alone, gigantic and solid, a solitary monolith with rounded edges.

How did such a rock arise from Earth? What is the geological explanation? The Aboriginal people have their explanations, myths that capture their spiritual connections with the place, a place that houses the spirits of their ancestors. And so the Rock is a sacred centre that sensitive visitors would do well not to climb or conquer as they might Mount Everest.

All geological, mythical, and biological explorations faded before the grandeur of the wonder, however, as we watched the Rock as the sun set. With each stage of the sunset, the Rock changed colour, from gold to orange to burning red to purple. The sun seemed to be setting inside the rock, Presence emanating from within.

In the end I was drawn into the wonder, into the Rock, aware only of Presence as an alluring mystery.

A Sacred Rock

I stood on a hill at sunset
overlooking a massive rock;
a mile high, some say,
and twenty miles around.

The rock was Uluru,
a golden boulder rising from deep in the red centre
of Australia,
a sacred site of Aboriginal peoples.
As I watched, the rock exuded wonder,
changing colour from instant to instant,
from celestial gold to earthy orange,
from vivid bronze to blazing red,
all the colours of a desert rainbow.

I sensed what many had sensed in other lands before me,
that point of spiritual concentration,
the navel of Earth
where spirit is incarnate in the soil
and the intrinsic worth of Earth is revealed.
Wonder in a rock
and in my consciousness.

At the other end of the spectrum of wonders are minute mysteries, moments when something quite tiny evokes that same sense of awe. When I was a boy, my brother and I used to collect bird's eggs and delight in their natural beauty. How many different colours might a magpie's egg be? we wondered.

On one occasion, as we wandered by a small stream, we noticed something unusual. What we discovered was the nest of a mistletoe bird. The nest was not located on top of some branches that would hold it in place, but was hanging from a branch like baby's bonnet suspended only a few inches from the surface of the water. The nest, moreover, was made mostly of wool intertwined with a few strands of grass. A delicate cradle indeed!

We wondered how such a tiny bird could make such a delicate hanging nest, where it found the wool, and how it survived, seated on a nest so close to the water. But all of those questions faded as we waded through the water and came close to that tiny wonder that still amazes me. Suffice it to say, that nest was too wonderful for us to touch and take an egg from.

These two illustrations of my encounters with wonder are rather dramatic. In reality, I am now aware of wonder in the honeyeaters that relish the nectar from my eucalyptus trees, in the rich red blossom of these same trees, and in the bees that compete for the nectar with the honeyeaters. In short, wonder is everywhere if we but have the consciousness to discern it. If Presence permeates everything, then Wonder can be discovered wherever that Presence is revealed to us.

Sustaining wonder

What sorts of things might we do to sustain wonder within ourselves, our community, and our Earth habitat? Sam Keen makes it clear that we need to sustain a sense of wonder to sharpen our awareness that this planet is a holy place. He writes,

To wonder is to perceive with reverence and love... and in wondering we come close to the feeling that the earth is holy. Historically the notion of wonder has been closely bound up with a religious mode of being in the world...in my experience, the substance of wonder is more frequently found in the prose of the secular than in the quaint poetry of religion...Whether we continue to talk about God is not so important as whether we retain the sense of wonder that keeps us aware that ours is a holy place (Keen, 1969, 211).

Keen's comments suggest that we can no longer stand by and watch what God has declared "wonder-full," and we have experienced as a sacred mystery of intrinsic worth, be treated as but a resource for humans to exploit. Nor can we ignore that, according to our biblical tradition, God made a covenant with Earth, making Earth a worthy partner. If we dare to consider the seven wonders identified by Job, we might also recognise that we should be committed to affirming the intrinsic worth and rights of each of these domains of nature.

All of us need to be conscious that Earth is a living planet, a fragile web of interconnected and interdependent forces and domains of existence, and a living community in which humans and all other life are kin who have a common heritage and destiny. The intrinsic wonder of this planet and all its interconnected mysteries must now be affirmed, and the right of all living entities (including Earth) to live fully must now be endorsed by legal, political, and religious bodies.

We also all need to be conscious that many domains of Earth are under threat and need protection. The welfare and rights of whales may be rightly championed by the likes of Greenpeace, but the intrinsic worth of all the hidden wonders deep in the ocean are rarely considered by most. Yet these realms, like many domains of the deep, are worthy of our concern and covenant concern. The rainforests are also under threat. Their worth is still measured by most in terms of their economic value. Yet they are a vital vehicle for absorbing carbon from the atmosphere. And now, after massive periods of drought, vast forests in the Amazon are dying. We need to speak for the trees.

The Covenant

Our covenant with Earth, therefore, needs to be more than to raise consciousness of the spiritual, the mysterious, and the wondrous in nature. We also need to be urging bodies to include a legal dimension that addresses the rights of all natural domains.

> *Given the mystery that all creation was created "very good" by God, who thereby affirmed its intrinsic worth and wonder (Genesis 1:31), we are invited to celebrate the intrinsic spiritual beauty of all the wonders we experience, to respect the integrity of creation, and protect the rights of all life and all domains of this planet.*

For each of us personally, however, a rich sense of wonder can be nurtured by taking time out to be in touch with nature, to be aware of wonder, and to be surprised by the spiritual in creation.

Let me suggest you come with me to the seashore looking out across the great Southern Ocean and wonder at the wonders before us. Behold again the ocean in endless motion! Wild waves keep roaring towards us, rising, falling, never still. Never!

The horizon far in the distance, alive with those same wild waters, seems still and silent, a long line where the infinite world of space meets the finite world of water, mystery meeting mystery. And if we move toward that horizon, that alluring distant point, wonder moves on and on ahead of us, so that we never actually sit on the horizon and enjoy a moment of rest. The horizon forever eludes us.

Or we look at the galaxy of sand granules at our feet, pebbles that may have come from rocks and deserts thousands of miles away and thousands of years ago. Between our toes, the wonder of sand in time and space teases our imagination and stirs our sense of wonder again.

Perhaps a pod of whales or dolphins swims by in harmony with the deep. Perhaps an albatross lands like a bird on skates and invites us to celebrate the sea. Perhaps a fairy penguin emerges from the water, after days in the deep, and calls to its baby in a burrow on the beach. The wonder of birdlife in the raging Southern Ocean leaves us speechless.

Conclusion

The mystery of wonder in nature confronted people like Job and many of our ancestors, just as it does each of us, if our consciousness is aroused.

As I reflect on wonder, it becomes apparent that we might well discern several dimensions of wonder.

First there are those bold wonders in nature that confront us directly. We are "wonderstruck" by the splendour, majesty, and stunning force of what we see. Nature breaks through and we are taken aback.

Often, however, wonder lies in the complexity of the mystery before us, in the hidden impulses that move the ocean, the deep memories that perpetuate life on the planet, the interplay of energies that enables galaxies to communicate.

Every wonder is ultimately an expression of intrinsic worth, a true value that is integral to the nature of the cosmos. Or in other words, we meet intrinsic wonder in the nature we see each day.

My own wondering is also a mystery, a response to the sacred I meet in nature, the wonders I celebrate.

Finally, then, I must ask whether wonder is not the very vehicle whereby Presence in creation reveals itself to me. If Presence permeates the planet, then surely one way Presence makes itself apparent is in the wonders that encapsulate the mysteries of the universe.

And if I wonder when I behold such wonders, then it would seem to me that my wonder is akin to worship! Come let us wonder together.

Blessing

May the wonders of this world
stun us with their splendour
until we appreciate
that their goodness is richer than gold
and ought to be preserved
as sacred treasure.
They are the original artwork of evolution
and the fingers of God.

Chapter Four

The Mystery of Life

❦

A Green Mystery

Keep your heart with all vigilance,
for from it flow the springs of life. (Proverbs 4:23)

Life

Life is a mystery that we can appreciate every morning when we wake and discover that we are alive – as are the birds calling from the trees, and the trees themselves.

All life is alive to the rest of the world in one way or another. Life impulses stimulate movement, communication, and expressions of vitality in all living creatures, from the simplest forms that live deep in the oceans to so-called advanced forms such as human beings.

Today we speak of the web of life, the way in which the various components of the cosmos interact and connect in order to enable all life to continue and evolve. The mystery of life is a mystery of deep beginnings and future connections.

We also connect life with spirit, that strong life impulse within Earth beings that offers more than mere existence. Spirit is not necessarily a discrete entity within a life form, but rather a driving inner force that links us in ways that are more than biological. As David Suzuki says,

> Beyond physical and social needs, we have yet another need, one that is vital to our long-term health and happiness. It is a need that encompasses all the rest, an aspect of human life that is so mysterious it is often disregarded or denied. Like air and water, like love and companionship of our kind, we need spiritual connection; we need to understand where we belong (Suzuki, 1997, 197).

Perhaps the deepest mystery of life, then, is the mystery of spirit, a green mystery we now explore as a dimension of the mystery of life.

Life in the Scriptures

The moment we begin to explore what the Scriptures say about the mystery of life, we discover that life is associated with the mystery of breathing. And the mystery of divine breathing is linked with the pulse of life. All life originates from the breath/spirit of God. Every inch of Earth is alive because of God's penetrating and enveloping breath. And the amazing thing about God's breath is that it blows all around us and we are not aware of the mystery enveloping us, entering us, animating us.

Another name for the breath of God is the atmosphere. Or as Theodore Hiebert's research reveals,

> *ruach*, the air of both atmospheric winds and animal respiration, is connected directly with God's being and God's activity in biblical thought. Air is not regarded as a material element of the natural world which, as a created substance, is empty of divinity. On the contrary, air as both atmospheric winds and breath is described in the Hebrew Scriptures as possessing a divine character. It originates from God, it is God's, it is a medium of revelation of God, and it is an indication of God's presence (2008, 13).

Once we appreciate from the Scriptures that Earth's atmosphere is indeed the breath of God, a number of texts begin to resonate as never before. We recall how God moulded the first human being out of orange clay and then breathed into his body the breath of life. That breath does not become some unique soul or spirit that is infused into humans. Rather that breath brings to life all the fauna and flora God has made. That same breath makes this planet green. In the Old Testament Scriptures the term for air, breath, and spirit is the same as the word for the wind that blows around. We all breathe the spirit of God...along with the trees.

The image of the divine artisan using mouth-to-mouth breathing to bring the first clay creature to life reminds us of a similar moment in the life of Elisha (2 Kings 4:32–35). When the son of the Shunammite woman dies, Elisha lies on top of the boy and gives him mouth-to-mouth breathing. Eventually the boy sneezes seven times and opens his eyes. It is not so much the miracle that resonates with me here, but an awareness that human breath is divine breathing and hence life-giving.

Life as celebration

Perhaps the biblical text about life that resonates most with me is Psalm 104. The celebration of life and the image of God enjoying life are provocative. The God who comes on the wings of the wind at the beginning of the Psalm turns out to *be* the wind, the very breath that animates life and landscape.

God's breathing surrounds Earth, enters Earth, and keeps Earth alive. The landscape of Earth is enlivened and flourishes because of the breath of God. The words of the Psalmist make that good news quite explicit: "You send forth your breath, and renew the face of the ground"(Psalm 104:30). Life is, in fact, a spiritual dimension of creation.

The Psalmist, however, not only wants to praise the Creator but encourages this penetrating breathing Presence to celebrate a living creation.

> May the presence of the Lord endure forever, and
> may the Lord rejoice in his works (Psalm 104:31).

The Psalmist sings of Leviathan, a creature specially formed for the Creator to play with (104:26). This suggests that we ought to discern dimensions of spiritual play and divine celebration in the many domains of nature, whether they be the cavorting of whales in the ocean or the dancing of dingoes in the desert.

The mystery of life, then, embraces both breathing and playing, both green grass and red wine:

> You cause the grass to grow for the cattle
> and plants for people to use,
> to bring forth food from the Earth,
> and wine to gladden the human heart,
> oil to make the face shine,
> and bread to strengthen the human heart (104:14–15).

The way of wisdom

Life is also a prominent theme in other wisdom books like Proverbs. While the orthodox mantra may have been that the "fear of the Lord is the beginning of wisdom," it is apparent that the wise sought the fullness of life by following the way of wisdom. As the wise say,

> She (wisdom) is a tree of life for those who lay hold
> on her;
> those who hold her fast are called happy
> (Proverbs 3:18).

> Wisdom is a fountain of life to one who has it;
> but folly in the punishment of fools (Proverbs 16:22).

Or as wisdom herself says,

> For whoever finds me finds life
> and obtains favour from the Lord (Proverbs 8:35).

The aim of the wise was to discern the imbedded laws of society and nature and learn to live by them. Life was to be lived in tune with nature. Life in this context was not merely existence as a human being, but the impulse to find meaning in the real world, to create good order and to celebrate being alive.

In the Hebrew Scriptures life may be a mystery, but the possibility of life after death is an even greater mystery. The writer of Ecclesiastes reminds us that humans and animals have the same breath and then asks, "Who knows then whether the human spirit goes upward and the spirit of the animal goes downward to the earth?" (3:19–21)

Regardless of what may happen after death, however, life here on Earth was viewed as a spiritual impulse from God, a gift to be celebrated and a reality dependent on the very breath of God animating each and every corner of creation.

Life in my tradition

In my tradition the integration of the natural and the spiritual dimensions of God in life tend to have been suppressed. The idea that the atmosphere was indeed the breath or the spirit of God was never really contemplated.

Life was generally divided into discrete domains of existence: temporal life and eternal life, human life and divine life. Life on Earth was temporary and fragile; life from God would ultimately mean heaven and eternal bliss.

Baptism was when a human being was first blessed with eternal life. Through that rite and the relevant faith of those involved, eternal life was infused into the child. Throughout its temporal life, the child would enjoy two lives – one that would end in death and another that would last forever. Non-human life in nature was devalued.

The eternal life of the individual was linked to the eternal soul within the temporary body. Body and soul were discrete entities. The Spirit of God was likewise quite separate from the natural world, even if it could influence lives on Earth. The suggestion that the atmosphere we breathe might in some way be identified with the breath or Spirit of God was considered ludicrous. The possibility that the air might in some way be considered a sacrament mediating the spiritual was never really contemplated.

The mystery of life and life after death in my tradition was grounded in the New Testament texts. The origins of life are associated with the Word, the creative power that precedes all creation and identified as the Second Person of the Trinity (John 1:4). Life in this context means an eternal presence, person, or power that precedes creation itself.

Throughout the gospel of John, Jesus is viewed as the source, mediator, and revelation of life as a spiritual dimension from God. Jesus is depicted as claiming to be the water of life, the bread of life, and the manifestation of life.

And life means eternal life. Whoever believes in Jesus as God's Son will enjoy eternal life and bodily resurrection. Even though Jesus performs miracles and heals the temporal bodies of human beings, his ultimate concern is apparently eternal life. Certainly it was portrayed this way in my tradition.

This portrayal of Jesus as the source of eternal life is linked with the theology of Saint Paul, who speaks of life after death as the ultimate mystery we must face. He believes that, in the twinkling of an eye, we will all one day be raised from the dead and assume imperishable forms that are not part of this world (1 Corinthians 15:51–54).

Another tradition prominent in the context of eternal life is the message of the book of Hebrews. Heaven, it seems, is portrayed as a better place, our true home above. We live on Earth longing for that better country where God resides with the angels (Hebrews 11:13–16). Life as reflected in nature is relegated to the margins. The inner life we possess, the one bound for heaven, should be the real focus of living.

The question we face then is whether the traditions of the Hebrew Scriptures or the Christian Church based on New Testament texts, are in any way consistent with the understanding of life revealed through ecology.

Life in nature

Ecology and evolution have radically transformed our understanding of life on this planet. We know Earth to be a component of the cosmos. We know the newly formed planet was pounded by meteors, the surface boiling because of the resulting friction, and lightning storms lasted millions of years until life was sparked somehow. As Bruce Sanguin reminds us,

The particular form of life that was sparked into being by the millions of years of lightning was bacteria. The fancy name for bacteria is *prokaryote*. It just means they don't have a nucleus. Their descendants the *eukaryotes*, out of which plants and animals emerge, are nucleated cells... We are now able to date the emergence of these *eukaryotes* to 2.45 billion years ago... And if you're beginning to wonder why you should worry about any of this, it might help to know that you wouldn't work without these little guys. They continue, in modified form, to be part of your own body (Sanguin 2007, 91, 93).

In other words, we are connected by bacteria to the emergence of life, to the beginnings of this mystery that now stirs our body, mind and consciousness. Beyond all the complex stages in the evolutionary process we are faced with the mysterious reality that through these billions of years of emergence, a deep life impulse has persisted and brought you and me to this moment in time – very much alive.

In the living planet we know today, all these bacteria and their descendants, in whatever form or stage of development, are all kin, all connected, all interrelated. We are a frenetic family of breeding bacteria, visiting and nurturing each other. As Suzuki says,

> No species exists in isolation from all others. In fact, today's estimated 30 million species are all connected through the intersection of their life cycles – plants depend on specific insect species to pollinate them, fish move through the vast expenses of the oceans feeding and being fed upon by other species, and birds migrate halfway around the world to raise their young on the brief explosion of insect populations in the Arctic. Together all species make up one immense web of interconnections that binds all beings to each other and the physical components of the planet (Suzuki, 1997, 137–138).

Suzuki also makes it clear that, whatever we may imagine about life after death, life and death are basic to the ecosystems of the planet.

Life and death form a balanced pair. It is a strange irony that death has been a critical instrument in the persistence of life. Humanity's age old dream of eternal life, if ever realised, would lock any species into an evolutionary straitjacket, eliminating the flexibility required to adapt to the planet's ever changing conditions. By allowing adaptive change to arise in successive generations, individual mortality enables species to survive over long periods of time (Suzuki, 1997, 137).

The processes of emergence, interconnection, and adaptive changes reach what we might consider a climax in the so-called eighth epoch of the universe story, with the emergence of human consciousness. Other forms of life may possess consciousness in one form or another, but the human, it seems, is the one life form that is truly conscious of its own consciousness. Through this consciousness, humans have reflected on their being, their origins, their identities, and the cosmos in which they live. They have become myth-makers, discerning dimensions of life that reach into unknown worlds. With this consciousness has come the mystery of imagination.

In almost every culture we meet myths about the origins of life, death, and the universe. Human consciousness of the spiritual or the sacred is found across cultures. Whether or not we explore the option of a "God impulse" hardwired into the brain, as Kevin Nelson has done, we are confronted with a human phenomenon: the belief in a spiritual dimension in the universe, a hidden life-giving impulse (Nelson, 2011).

For example, in the Judaic Hassid tradition, God fashions a very large clay vessel and then breathes the fire of love into it. God's breath is so powerful that the clay vessel explodes into billions of particles, each of which contains an original God spark. Our challenge, it is said, is to fan that spark into a flame (Cowley, 2011, 6).

The question I now ask, in the light of ecology and contemporary human consciousness, is whether that spiritual dimension is the very core of the evolutionary process, an integral impulse of nature, or whether it is a discrete Spirit – be it called the Holy Spirit, the Rainbow Spirit, or the Cosmic Spirit. Is this primal spark ignited from within the cosmos, or is it the deliberate act of a separate igniting spirit outside the cosmos?

Denis Edwards also seeks to come to terms with spirit as the Holy Spirit and as the Life-Giver in the context of evolution and ecology. He, however, argues that,

> the Spirit is not a power that can be discovered among the forces of the universe. The laws and forces of nature have their own integrity. The action of the Life-Giver is at another level... The Spirit of God is the Life-Giver, the power of becoming, who enables the unfolding of the universe and the evolution of life on Earth (Edwards, 1999, 90–91).

For Denis Edwards (and most in the Christian tradition) there is a separate life-giving power. In recent times, that life-giving impulse has been recognised as immanent in creation and, for scholars like Denis Edwards, deep in the evolutionary process. I wonder, however, whether in the evolution of our consciousness, we humans have focused with such intensity on the human life we have inherited that we have transformed its source into another being outside our world.

What if, then, I recognise that the Life-Giving Impulse in this universe is the spiritual core of the cosmos, part of our biological heritage, our cosmic identity, our human consciousness? What if the spiritual is part and parcel of the geological, the biological, and the cosmological – that the life impulse is indeed the Life Impulse? What if, instead of seeking the source of life out there or back then in some other being or force, we find Life here and now, deep within, pulsing throughout our planet?

Life in my world

Time and again I have been experienced moments filled with an intense presence of spirit. On one occasion, while visiting an African American church in St. Louis, Missouri, people were being "smitten by the Spirit." The person next to me was smitten and suddenly convulsed on the ground beside me. Then the mother of the preacher, one among the choir before us, fell down before the congregation, who praised God in response. The people involved believed that their experiences were a result of the Spirit imparting ecstasy to their lives.

On another occasion, I was privileged to be part of a Christian fertility rite for a woman who wanted healing. Until that moment she had not been able to become pregnant. She wanted life to be stirred within her. The rite was a Eucharist focusing on the healing blessing promised in Holy Communion. Within weeks of that rite, the mother was pregnant; in the eyes of all involved, the Spirit had stirred life in her womb.

Regardless of how we may interpret such experiences, my experiences of the spirit of life have taken place in domains of nature. As I enter a given domain I wonder whether I can experience the mystery of that habitat, whether I can feel the pulse or pulses of nature in that location, whether I can be conscious of the spiritual as part of the natural.

I may wander through a community of trees and listen to the breezes blowing through the leaves. I feel the movement of the wind and sense the breath of Life in the air, among the trees and in the lungs. For the trees of the forest are the lungs of Earth. I am aware of the wind, breath, and atmosphere – the spirit we associate with God. It animates us and all life on Earth.

The Breath of God

Time and again as a boy
I wandered through the bush,
caressing the green moss on myrtles hundreds of years old,
tasting the soft gum of blooming wattles,
smelling the aroma of crushed eucalyptus leaves,
hearing country music in the surrounding air.
Then one day, as if by revelation,
what I was reading about God's spirit came to life.
I breathed in time with the trees,
in tune with the breeze,
inhaling deeply.
I was breathing the breath of God
as Adam had done in the forest of Eden.
The air, the wind,
the atmosphere
were the very breath of God, the Spirit
that animates me and every tree in every age.
I was in Eden.

Other times, I explore being in tune with the ground beneath my feet. I recognise Earth as a planet pulsing with
millions of life impulses, each encapsulating the mystery of
life. And I wonder whether I may, perhaps, feel the pulse of
Earth through one of her manifold life forms. I pause to feel
the pulse of Earth.

The Pulse of Earth

In my mind
I now know that Earth is alive
pulsing
deep within the core
and across the crust,
a vibrating mass of living matter.

But how do I feel the pulse of Earth?
Can I put my finger on throbbing extremities,
or connect with the life forces
and hidden impulses
that permeate this planet?

If I hold a wild flower in my fingers,
place my hands on the trunk of a tree,
touch the beak of a pelican
or grasp a silver eel,
will I feel the pulse of Earth?

The impulses to live,
to sing,
to express wonder,
are in every throbbing cell of our planet.

Finally
I begin to feel the pulse of Earth
with my hands in the air
my feet in the ground
my spirit embracing
the throb of life
in every murmur
of mystery.

Of course, the message that life is mystery can happen at any time and any place, if one is aware of the pulses of nature interacting in celebration.

Celebrating Life

Recently, two laughing kookaburras
perched on the eucalyptus trees
on either side of my house.
In the dusk they began laughing
in dialogue
communicating with each other
– or perhaps with me –
peals of laughter
echoing through the valley.

The Aboriginal people of Queensland
have a tradition
that kookaburras are signals of good news
for all who can hear.

If the Psalmist thought God created Leviathan
to sing and play with,
I wonder whether
I might discern
that the primal Life Impulse,
the Spirit deep in the land Down Under,
created the kookaburra
to provoke us to laugh
and celebrate life.

Sustaining life

Many thinkers today urge us to explore the mystery of life.
The depth of life may be experienced as a spiritual dimension
to be celebrated. Bishop Spong describes his search as follows.

> My search for "heaven" will cause me to turn to this
> life, to its very depths, for that is the only place where
> I now believe we can hear the echoes of eternity. In
> that search I believe, we will discover that the word
> "heaven" points not to something external to us, but
> to something that is part of us (Spong, 2009, 143).

One way to help sustain the mystery of life on our planet is to become aware of the atmosphere as being more than air. If we dare to wander among the trees of a forest and listen to the breezes flowing through the leaves, we may well become conscious of that spiritual life-giving impulse that enables humans to breathe, the trees to sing, and the undergrowth to quiver with life.

I invite you to feel the movement of the wind and sense the breath of God in the air, among the trees and in the lungs. Be aware that the wind, breath, and atmosphere are all God's spirit. It animates us and all life on Earth.

We, like all creatures and all that is green on our planet, are dependent on the breath of life, the spirit we may call God. If we dare to make a covenant with Earth, our mission is to become agents of healing intent on keeping our habitat green and sustaining life in all its forms.

The Covenant

Given the mystery that the air/breath of God animates the face of Earth and all life on Earth (Psalm 104:30) we are invited to hear and feel the breath of God animating us and all life, and we are called to sustain Earth as a green planet by preserving all species of fauna and flora.

One of many examples of how people are healing parts of the planet and restoring the green is in Western Australia, where vast areas of wooded lands were cleared and became saline, unable to support animals or crops. Now concerned locals are seeking to heal the saline soil by using their skills in biology and agriculture. They are replanting the saline soils with plants native to the area and finding the natural materials needed to restore the ground to its original fertility. With this kind of care, the salt plains are coming back to life.

Conclusion

The mystery of life deep within nature challenges us. Throughout all the ecosystems of the universe life emerged and we, by the grace of the cosmos, are conscious of life in us and our planet.

The more I reflect on this mystery of life as we know and experience it on Earth, the more I discover spiritual dimensions to it. One such dimension is the biblical tradition where the atmosphere, the very breath we inhale, is known as the breath or spirit of God. In this tradition, the spiritual had long been understood to be part of the natural.

We know that through the process of evolution, trillions of forms of matter have come to life. Just as amazing, however, is that consciousness of this life has evolved within us.

From the depths of the cosmos, it seems, the impulse for life to emerge was latent, hidden within the chemicals and black holes of the universe.

And that life impulse – or Life Impulse in sacred terms – is the spiritual force we sense and celebrate in every green leaf, every orange patch of lichen, and every swirling silver fin. Life emerges in every flower, every ant, and every batch of bacteria.

If this Life Impulse reaches deep into the past, I wonder what role my bacteria will be playing in the emerging consciousness of beings in the future – a thousand years from now or more. Or is that eternal Life?

Blessing

May the atmosphere,
the moist breath of God enveloping us,
penetrate every pore of our planet
and activate all those impulses needed
to keep our forests green,
our swallows singing,
and our dragonflies dancing.

Chapter Five

The Mystery of Voice

A Blue Mystery

They made the land a desolation;
it mourns to me. (Jeremiah 12:11)

Voice

The voice of nature is a mystery few seem to hear. Bird voices often sing in the forest, but the voice of the forest is rarely the focus of attention. Animal voices may be heard in the fields, but the voice of the field is ignored, and the music of the wind goes unnoticed.

We need to listen to the voices of Earth and her domains, whether they are heard as songs of celebration or cries of anguish, whether they praise God or lament their lot. Yet so often these voices are not taken seriously.

We need to acknowledge the suffering that the environmental crisis causes. We need to empathise with Earth, earth domains, and all Earth beings, and learn to hear their cries as well as sing with them in celebration.

The diverse voices of Earth form another mystery of nature, and we are called to articulate those voices to our community. We need to be prophets for our mother Earth and for our kin in creation.

I associate the colour blue with the primal waters, the source of the great Flood, and the domain where Jonah was cast. Like the land, the seas roar and the deep utters its voice. The sea monsters and the deep also praise God. The groaning of creation emanates from within the deep.

Join me as we open our ears, our hearts, and our deep sensing to the sounds, songs, and sufferings of our planet, and recognise their spiritual dimension.

Voice in the Scriptures

The Old Testament prophets, such as Jeremiah, frequently record how they hear the voices of Earth and the domains of Earth crying to God in agony. Shirley Wurst retrieves the voice of Earth in her voiced reading of Jeremiah 4 (2001, 176ff). The poignant end of that chapter (Jeremiah 4:19–28) illustrates the anguish in the voices of both Jeremiah and Earth.

> **Earth** *(her emotion is apparent in her voice; she is about to be abused)*:
> My anguish! My anguish!
> I writhe in pain!
> O the walls of my heart!
> My heart is beating wildly;
> I cannot keep silent;
> for I hear the sound of the trumpet,
> the alarm of war.

> **Jeremiah** *(Jeremiah is watching what is happening and is powerless to do anything)*:
> Disaster overtakes disaster,
> Earth is laid waste.

> **Earth** *(it is obvious as she speaks that her body is shuddering from the pain of the blows as her body is beaten, her clothes torn)*:

Suddenly my tents are destroyed,
my curtains in a moment.
How long must I see the standard,
and hear the sound of the trumpet?

Jeremiah (*speaking to the audience, describing what he is witnessing; the compassion and the pain are apparent in his voice*):
I looked at Earth, and lo, she was wasted and void;
and to her skies, and they had no light.
I looked on her mountains, and lo, they were
    quaking,
and all the hills moved to and fro.
I looked, and lo, there was no life at all
and all the birds of the air had fled.
I looked, and lo, fruitful Earth was a desert,
and Judah and Israel were laid in ruins
before YHWH, before YHWH's fierce anger.

YHWH (*there is a hint of regret in YHWH's voice; YHWH recognises what YHWH has done, but cannot empathise with the violated Earth; YHWH now focuses on Israel and Judah*):
Earth shall be a desolation;
yet I will not make a full end.
Because of this Earth shall mourn,
and her skies above grow black;
for I have spoken, I have purposed;
I have not relented nor will I turn back.

Jeremiah speaks for Earth and gives voice to her experience of desolation and abuse. He knows too that God is aware of Earth's cries of anguish, her deep mourning and despair.

Earth suffers because of humanity's actions. And we would ask today whether we can hear the voice of planet Earth mourning. Can we hear her heart beating wildly in fear because of how humans make many domains desolate and barren? And where are the prophets like Jeremiah, to give voice to the cries of Earth?

The Psalms, however, focus on celebration and praise. Psalm 65:12–13, for example, reads,

The pastures of the wilderness shout for joy,
the hills gird themselves with rejoicing.
The pastures are clothed with flocks,
and the valleys cover themselves with grain,
they shout for joy, indeed they sing.

In the past, Earth's voice in the Bible has been taken as poetic metaphor and not as a significant voice of nature. The Earth Bible team argues that such metaphors embrace a living dimension of truth and that it is no less problematic to speak of the voice of Earth than to speak of the voice of God (2001, 24).

Perhaps the most powerful expression of the voice in nature in the Scriptures is found in Romans 8. Here that voice is described as creation groaning (Romans 8:19–25). The good news in this passage is astounding. Creation is groaning, like a woman in childbirth, as she awaits the rebirth of

Earth. The Spirit of God is also groaning with creation on our behalf.

The Sighing Spirit

Can you hear me sighing
deep sighs,
sighing to God on Earth's behalf, on your behalf?
I am the Spirit, the soul of creation.
I am groaning with creation,
yearning to be free of the burden of past curses
and current crimes against nature.
I am sighing, crying to God for Earth
to be heard and healed,
for her pain to become joy,
her groans to become birth-pangs.
Can you hear me sighing,
hear creation groaning, Earth crying
with the hope of a new day?
Please listen with me
and sigh with me.

I might not feel happy about the way God of the prophets treats nature. Books like Ezekiel are full of "grey" texts that have God destroying parts of nature, even though nature is quite innocent of any crime. Yet I can empathise with a prophet like Jeremiah who hears Earth moaning, mourning, and screaming to God because of the desolation she suffers at the hands of God and humans. Such texts invite me to listen to those spiritual impulses of nature that reflect the agony of Earth caused by human abuse.

Voice in my tradition

In the past, partly due to the influences of the Enlightenment and modern science, the voices of Earth and the various domains of creation have been silent in my tradition. Earth and creation are not considered living entities with voices to be heard. They are inanimate and devoid of intellect or emotion. They are not subjects. They have not evolved the way humans have, with reason and consciousness. And so they have no voice.

The many biblical references to land, sea, forests, or fauna lamenting their plight have been interpreted as irrelevant poetic metaphors. The focus has been on the needs and voices of humans, not those of nature. Rarely have interpreters sought to hear the voice of Earth; her voice has been blocked out by the voices of humans. But Earth has a voice that ought to be heard as we listen with a new awareness of our intimate connection with the rest of creation.

Romans chapter 8 has rarely been associated with Earth's current environmental crises. In my tradition, as I recall, creation groaning as a woman in childbirth was linked to the end of the world, when there will be a new heaven and a new Earth. But the curses caused by our current abuse of creation cannot be ignored. Nor can the voice of Earth groaning and the Spirit in Earth sighing in the hope that we will empathise with creation.

It has also been traditional to view creation as inanimate, as voiceless matter. But as noted above, many of the prophets heard the voices of Earth and the various domains of Earth. If we today were to identify with the domains named in biblical narratives, we might also hear the cries that have been suppressed because of our dualistic view of nature. As Earth beings we need to listen anew to the groaning of creation.

Imagine if we were part of the story of the Flood. What voices might we hear? The voices of the innocent Earth creatures destroyed in the Flood? The voice of Earth herself devastated by the waters of chaos? The voices of the forests inundated by water for twelve long months? Can we hear creation groaning beneath the floodwaters? *Why me? What have I done to deserve this?* Can we hear the cosmos groaning when the fountains of the primordial deep erupt and the oceans above the sky inundate Earth below?

Wally Fejo, an Australian Aboriginal, invites us to take a second look at the presence of God in the Flood. For him, God is not a being outside creation, but deep within.

> God is not at some distance on some cloud watching the Flood with an expression of justified anger. God is in Earth. God experiences the Flood, the death of life on Earth. The suffering of God in the Flood anticipates the suffering of God in the crucifixion (2000, 142).

In my tradition, the voice to be heard was the voice of God articulated through the preacher speaking for God from the Word of God in the Bible. To ascribe any value or authority to a voice from nature was tantamount to paganism. To suggest that the voice of God might be mediated through nature was just as unacceptable. Earth had no voice that deserved serious attention.

Voice in nature

Ecology has now revealed that not only are all ecosystems interrelated, but that the elements, entities, and beings of these systems communicate. We quoted Berry in the Introduction to the effect that "every being has its own voice. Every being declares itself to the whole universe. Every being enters into communion with other beings" (1999, 4).

Planet Earth, then, is a lively community of beings that interact and communicate. And science, it seems, is beginning to appreciate these modes of communication, most of which may be unheard by the human ear. As Suzuki says,

> Our view of the world is created by the degree of sensitivity of our sensory organs... Insects can respond to a single molecule of pheromone floating in the air. Our ears lack the ability to detect the high-pitched sounds that help bats manoeuvre, capture prey and avoid predators. We are deaf to the low-pitched frequencies that are the songs of marine leviathans echoing through oceans halfway round the world (1997, 139).

Nature is replete with myriad voices echoing through the planet. The mystery before us is whether the cries of these voices reflect a deeper voice. Are the voices emanating from Earth an expression of the voice of Earth herself? Is the voice of Earth, in its many manifestations, the innate spirit of Earth? Is that spirit a dimension of God?

We may explore the mystery of voice by returning to the Australian Aboriginal worldview set out in the *Rainbow Spirit Theology*, where the elders include a chapter entitled "Land and Crying." The chapter is acutely sensitive to the voice of the land violated and desecrated by European invaders. The elders listen to the landscape. They cite, for example, the pollution of Maralinga (a nuclear testing site on the Nullarbor Plain in South Australia) caused by the fallout from British atomic bomb tests.

The elders hear that the land is crying because spiritual bonds have been broken, the sacred stories have been forgotten, the life-forces in the land are not bringing forth rich vegetation, and because the Aboriginal custodians have been torn from the land (1997, 42–47).

Significantly, the elders are also aware that the crying of the land is accompanied by the crying of the Creator Spirit.

> The Creator Spirit is crying because the blood of Aboriginal people has desecrated the land. The land is crying out because the blood on the ground has not been heard, and the sacrifice of those who died has not been remembered (1997, 48).

To hear and understand the voice of Earth – the land, the forests, the waters – we need to learn the language of the land. The suffering of the land, says Yunupingu, is communicated to those who know the language of the land.

> Even when I am not on my tribal land I am able to speak sign language; just like people do who don't speak each other's language. I do the same thing by looking at the hills with no trees. I understand that maybe those hills are suffering a bit. I understand that Mother Earth is suffering because there is so much devastation. Trees are dying and have to be cleared away, lands are being cut by floodwaters, and many other types of environmental destruction are taking place. That is when you experience the suffering of the Spirit of the Land because of the carelessness of the non-Aboriginal; people who call themselves the "owners" of this country (1996, 9–10).

Earth's cries have also been heard by those working in uranium mines where land has been rendered vile and sterile by the toxic outflows. Her cries reach the heart and soul of sensitive women surrounded by apparently heartless mining companies. As we listen, we may well hear the cry of one such Aboriginal woman, Mary Duroux.

My mother, my mother, what have they done?

Crucified you like the Only Son!
Murder committed by mortal hand!
I weep, my mother, my mother, the land (1992, 20).

It seems to me that by bringing together the insights of ecology and the memories of these elders, we can recognise that Earth and that Presence we call God are deeply connected. If we dare to hear the voice of Earth groaning in our world, we may recognise that voice as one with the Spirit groaning, as Paul implies in the version of Romans 8 above. Rainbow Spirit Elders know how to listen to country. It is time all other humans did the same. Or in the words of Thomas Berry,

> In the opening years of the 21st century we need to renew our intimacy with our local bioregion and with the North American continent but also with the planet Earth itself, in its comprehensive extent and the diversity of its component regions (1999, 89).

I applaud the call to become intimate with specific locations and indeed the whole planet. I would suggest, however, that we need to go beyond the "total earth science" that Berry recommends for achieving this goal. I believe we also need to use our senses and feel the pains of specific bioregions and hear the voices of regions abused by human greed and ignorance.

Voice in my experience

It is especially through my association with Aboriginal Australians that I have learned to listen to land and sea, forest and field. I discovered their profound capacity to connect with the spirit of the landscape, the soul of the desert, and the dreaming in sites or song-lines. In short, they could hear the voice of Earth emanating from many locations and in many forms. And where Earth had been abused they could hear her cry.

Call of Country

We arrive at the dry reaches of Maralinga,
a desolate, desecrated,
and forsaken site.
Here darkness once covered the land
with a thick cloud of death.
We cross the broken fence that warns
of radioactive fallout still alive
long after the atomic blasts of the 1950s.

We meet a few Aboriginal people
returning to the fringes of the bomb sites
on what was once sacred soil.

Why are you returning to country?
Why?
"Because our country is calling us,
crying to be healed."

We ask them whether their suffering –
from the fallout, the forced removals,
and the wounding of their lands –
was worth the sacrifice.
After all, the politicians said,
"We need this land to test these bombs
that keep the world free."

And they reply,
"They crucified this land
and she is not free.
She is crying deep within,
hoping for a chance to live again."
(Habel, 1999, 180)

While I was in India exploring the issues of global warming
and climate change, I experienced the groanings of ocean
and land in a way I never expected. The voice of a landscape now flooded by sea still haunts me.

Groaning in Hope

I stood on the shore in the Bay of Bengal,
South of Calcutta, in rural India.
A few hundred metres out to sea a sandbar gleamed,
shining golden in the summer sun.
On the shore local fishermen
cast their nets for their daily catch.
"See that sand bar," said a local fisherman.
"It was a village only a few years ago."
In the silence that followed,
I could hear creation groaning, deep in the sea,
groaning in hope that we would listen
and repent.

It might appear that hearing the cries of Earth or the voice of nature in various domains of our planet is a special gift available only to poets or prophets. For me, however, it is also a spiritual experience, one of tuning the inner ear of my spirit to the music of Mother Earth, whether that be a dark lament or a symphony of hope, a violent scream or a joyous song.

Sustaining the mystery of voice

It is easy to be pessimistic about the crises facing our environment, to throw up our hands in frustration, and to place the responsibility on our politicians or scientists. But the good news that arises from this rainbow mystery is that we who hear the groaning of creation can make a difference. We are summoned, like the prophets of old, to confront and comfort, to represent Earth and the creatures of Earth to all in our community. That is our mission.

To do this, we have to learn to listen to the lands, the oceans, the forests, and the ground. We need to hear the many voices of Earth and recognise that they are a mystery, an expression of the soul of Earth, a spiritual force to be heard and not suppressed.

Significantly, in all the literature about eco-theology, eco-ethics, and eco-spirituality, there is extended discussion about the spiritual, the sacred, and the presence of God mediated through nature. Very few authors, however, focus on Earth as a subject whose voice we have the capacity to hear and heed. There is great emphasis on viewing nature and responding with wonder. There is very little about hearing nature and responding with a call for justice or hope. For me, a spiritual connection with creation is one of acute sensitivity that discerns the spiritual with ears, head, and heart. We need to hear the voice of Earth as well as behold the wonders of Earth.

Following the cue of Yunupingu cited above, we probably need to learn the language of the land to be able to hear the voice of the land. Barren landscapes express cries of despair. The voice of polluted streams is almost choked with waste and poisons. The language of extreme weather conditions speaks forcefully of global warming if we are ready to listen.

One way of raising our awareness of this spiritual force crying for justice is to visit places where human greed and folly have led to the destruction of forests, fields, and waterways. Wading in waters filled with waste or walking through fields turned into saltpans can help raise our consciousness and open us to Earth's cries of pain. Sometimes it is even worth lying with an ear to the barren ground and listening to her groaning.

On September 1, 2011, I stood on the hill of the Australia War Memorial at Villers-Bretonneux in France. From that hill one can see the trenches once inhabited by soldiers from many divisions – French, English, Australian, Canadian, and German. The entire scene was a battlefield for some four years during the Great War.

Across those few hundred acres during the course of the war, about four million humans and eight million horses died. The memorial is a testimony to the scorched Earth – and dare I say, scorched life – policy that characterised that war and many wars that followed.

That memorial records the names of the thousands of Australian lives that were lost, whether they were Jewish,

Christian, Muslim, or agnostic. But where is there a memorial to all the non-human lives that were lost? Where is there a memorial to all the fallen horses, trees, and birds – all in the name of human dominion over a small piece of Earth?

As I listened in silence, I could hear the cries of all who suffered – humans, animals, and landscape. The scorched Earth metaphor might sound like a surface experience. For me, however, the cries came from deep in the trenches, from the craters, from Earth's very soul.

Scorched Earth. Screaming Earth. What an appropriate way to describe what human greed and violence have perpetrated in recent years, using everything from nuclear weapons to polluting gases, from deforestation to deadly poisons. What if we were to identify a series of scorched Earth sites around the planet and erect memorials to the sacrifices of Earth? Such scorched Earth sites might make us ready to hear the voices of Earth and our non-human kin rather than suppressing or denying them.

The Covenant

We need to hear whatever cries we may hear also as cries of hope, the yearning of Earth for healing and new birth. And central to that hope is that we humans will take responsibility for our actions, past and future. Accordingly, we would do well to consider our covenant obligation.

Given the mystery that all creation is groaning, from the ocean depths to the ozone layer (Romans 8:18–25), we are invited to empathise with the cries of Earth and the groaning of creation and we are called, as the prophets of old, to proclaim publicly, on Earth's behalf, the pains and hopes of our planet.

Conclusion

The mystery of voice rising from Earth is one that has not stirred our consciousness as much as other mysteries of the cosmos. Yet, the voices of many domains of nature are frequently reflected in the biblical tradition, even if they are often treated by scholars as irrelevant poetry.

Ecology makes it abundantly clear that components of a given eco-system are not only interrelated, but communicate in a variety of ways, even if their modes of communication do not correspond to what we humans call language. The voices of nature do not need to be articulated as human language to be valid and vital.

From our Aboriginal brothers and sisters, we can learn the language of nature by listening to the landscape and hearing the voice of Earth as a subject with spiritual impulses.

It is especially important that we learn to hear the cries of this planet that is suffering from the wounds caused by human efforts to dominate nature, and address this suffering. This voice of Earth crying because of environmental degradation recalls the groaning of creation recognised by Saint Paul in his letter to the Romans.

In the last analysis, I believe the voice of Earth is a mystery we might call soul or spirit. Earth has soul and urges us to hear her lament. We are called to be prophets who give voice to the injustice suffered by Earth.

Blessing

May the groaning of creation,
deep and blue and bold,
penetrate our smothered consciousness,
until we become prophets of Earth,
giving voice to her injustices
and supporting her spirit.

Chapter Six

The Mystery of Wisdom

An Indigo Mystery

Where can wisdom be found?
Where is the locus of discernment?
(Job 28:12)

Wisdom

Wisdom is another mystery that leaves me shuddering with amazement. In his exploration of the psychological roots of wisdom, Stephen Hall defines wisdom as a special human capacity to integrate the cognitive, the affective, and the reflective (2010, chapter 3). In my understanding, however, wisdom is a mystery that challenges my spirit as well as my mind. It is a dimension of reality far deeper than profound knowledge or superior understanding. To me, wisdom is a mystery that reaches back to the origin of the cosmos.

Wisdom may also include the way our ancestors discerned the sacred in the interconnectedness of the forces of nature. Those very forces, I would argue, also reflect what we might identify as wisdom in nature.

My task then is to explore the mystery of wisdom and how I might discern wisdom in nature.

Wisdom in the Scriptures

In the Scriptures there is a cluster of texts referred to as wisdom literature. These texts include the books of Proverbs, Job, and Ecclesiastes. There are similar wisdom texts in other ancient Near Eastern cultures. In the broadest sense of the term, the wise were like the scientists of the ancient world, intent on discerning knowledge by intense observation of nature or society.

Have you ever wondered why a frog always jumps like a frog and never runs like an ant? Have you ever been fascinated by the way a baby bird learns to fly rather than swim like an eel? There is something inbuilt in each creature that enables it to be true to its nature.

Scientists have examined this phenomenon and sought to explain it in terms of genetics or ecosystems. Each creature, it seems, has an inbuilt genetic code that governs how it lives, moves, and reproduces. Quite remarkably, the differences between the genetic coding in a human being and that of any other animal are relatively few. Yet these inner codes determine that a snake moves in a way quite distinct from that of a snail or an eagle or a human.

In the ancient world, the wise used a number of terms in reference to this inner code. The most explicit term is "the way" (*derek* in Hebrew). Because the term "way" has a wide range of meanings in English, the technical meaning of this term is easily overlooked in translation. We can speak of a way of doing things without having a specific technical modus operandi in mind. And in wisdom literature the term can also be used generally in reference to the ways of the wicked or the ways of the righteous.

The term "way" (*derek*) has a technical sense (Habel, 2003, 286). It refers to the inner code of behaviour that characterizes a phenomenon of the natural world. The way of something reflects its essential character, its instinctual nature, its internal impulse. So the way of an eagle is to soar across the sky and with its eagle eye discern prey far below. The way of a snake is to slither across rocks and camouflage its presence in the grass.

In this usage, *derek* refers to the driving characteristic of a given entity. Perhaps the German equivalent (from Kant) is the term *bildende Kraft* (a term used by scientists seeking to classify creatures such as the platypus). Every phenomenon of nature has its *bildende Kraft*, its own inner formative force, or as I suggest, its driving characteristic (Eco, 2000, 93). This concept of *derek* is crucial, I believe, for an understanding of a basic wisdom cosmology.

In this tradition, it is a major task of the person interested in becoming wise to observe nature and understand its "ways" closely. In so doing, the individual may not learn only about the phenomenon itself, but also about life. The novice is encouraged to watch the ant, observe the distinctive code of behaviour found in ants, and so gain some wisdom.

> Go to the ant, you lazybones!
> Consider its way and be wise!
> Without having any chief
> or officer or ruler,
> it prepares its food in summer,
> and gathers its sustenance in harvest
> (Proverbs 6:6–8).

Here the wise teacher is leading a youth to analyse the "way" or "ways" of an ant! What characterizes an ant? What makes an ant an ant? What is the code or "way" of an ant? If you figure out that mystery you have gained some insight into wisdom!

The way or code that is typical of the nature of ants is for them to function as a corporate body without any hierarchy – without any bosses or leaders – a mystery that modern scientists still find fascinating. Another code that is true of ants is their instinctual capacity to gather food in summer and store it for the winter.

The ancient wise were committed to observing phenomena and discerning their nature. The verb "to discern" *(bin)* might be translated "to research through close examination." The person with the necessary cognitive skills of discernment could discover the "code" or "way" *(derek)* of the object being examined. Such was the task of the wise, a task we may well wish to emulate as species disappear and their "ways" on our planet become extinct. This mystery can be defined as follows.

> Fundamental to the mystery of wisdom in nature is that every phenomenon and domain of nature has an innate code *(derek)* or law that governs its characteristic behaviour as an integral part of an ecosystem.

There is, however, an even deeper dimension to wisdom in these Scripture texts. Of special significance is Job 28, which raises the ancient question: Where is wisdom found?

Humans may probe the depths of Earth for precious metals and other hidden things, but the locus or "place" of wisdom in the cosmos remains a mystery. "Place" (*maqom*) is a technical expression referring to the locus of a phenomenon or domain in a given ecosystem of the cosmic order. The ultimate question is the "place" of wisdom herself in the cosmos. Clearly, wisdom is not seen here as a body of past knowledge, or a deep level of understanding, or the accumulated tradition of the wise elders. Wisdom is a prior determinative reality in a mysterious "place."

It is apparent from the wisdom literature that wisdom is hidden. The deep claims, "it is not in me"; the birds of the air cannot detect it; the land of death has only heard a rumour of it. In this wisdom literature, God is the one who knows its "place." But God's knowledge of the place of wisdom is not some innate divine capacity. God, like a true scientist of old, observes all the phenomena on Earth, examines all the domains under the sky, and in the process discerns the locus of wisdom in the cosmos.

> But God discerned her way,
> and came to know her place.
> For God looked to the ends of Earth
> and saw everything under the sky (Job 28:23–24).

And where does God specifically look? God searches those domains of nature we would connect with climate – the wind, the waters, the storms, and the rain. And, significantly, God makes this close examination when creating these various domains and establishing their nature. So wisdom is connected with the process of creation from the beginning.

Just as significant here is that God does not simply observe these domains of nature, but focuses on their several codes, described variously as the force/weight of the wind, the volume/measure of the waters, the rule for the rain, and the way of the thunderstorm. The codes provide the clue to something more, something deeper, something all-encompassing, namely wisdom. These codes of creation connect with the hidden design, the inspiring blueprint that determines their nature. Behind all the codes of the climate is a dynamic blueprint called wisdom!

> When God fixed the weight of the wind
> and meted out the waters by measure,
> when God made a rule for the rain
> and the way of the thunderstorm,
> then God saw her [wisdom] and appraised her,
> established her and probed her
> (Job 28:25–27, my translation).

When God discovers the hidden mystery of wisdom at the core of creation, the divine Sage checks and double-checks the finding. She is appraised and probed. In the process, wisdom is "established" as the ultimate blueprint govern-ing the codes of creation. Here wisdom is not an attribute of God but a deep dimension of the cosmos connected with the codes in creation, the creative impulses that generate the cosmos. Wisdom is the code that integrates the various codes in nature, and governs the ultimate ecosystem (that also governs the weather patterns of the world).

> Wisdom (*kochma*) then is also the underlying design of the cosmos, a dynamic blueprint that orders, gov-erns, and integrates the various codes and systems in the diverse ecosystems of the cosmos.

The preceding interpretation of Job 28 provides a basis for re-examining the famous wisdom poem of Proverbs 8:22–31, where wisdom presents herself as a companion of God at the time of creation. The rendering of the opening verse of the poem is crucial to an appreciation of God's relationship with wisdom. A literal translation, I believe, is the most enlightening (Habel 2003, 294).

> **YHWH acquired me first,**
> **his way before his works.**
> **From of old, from antiquity I was established,**
> **from the first, from the beginnings of Earth**
> **(Proverbs 8:22–23, my translation).**

The verb here translated "acquired" (*qana*) is the standard term employed in Proverbs for acquiring wisdom (as in 4:3, 7).

The repeated injunction of the teacher is to "acquire wisdom!" Given this context, it seems logical to understand this term in the standard way rather than seek a relatively obscure meaning of "create" from other contexts such as Genesis 14:19. Moreover, the precedent of Job 28 makes it clear that God, as Sage, may be understood to discover wisdom as an existing or emerging reality in the world. It is also evident from verses 24 and 25 of Proverbs 8 that wisdom "emerges" prior to creation. She is not created by God, but embraced by God.

Also important is the translation of *derek* in its technical sense of "way" or code. To render *derek* by the term "work" as in the NRSV is to completely conceal the differentiation between the "way/code" of something and the making of something. Wisdom claims to be the "way" that precedes the work, the creative activity of God. This priority of wisdom as the way is apparent throughout the poem. Wisdom is not a "work" of God, but a prior presence and force.

What then is the function of wisdom as the "way" that precedes and accompanies God at creation? Clearly wisdom is more than a friendly companion. In Job 28, a clue may lie in how the various domains of creation are described. In some verses, the focus seems to be on the domain itself. In others, however, wisdom announces her presence prior to its code, its way, being established. Wisdom, like the blueprint in Job 28, seems to be the dynamic design that inspires God and determines the various codes of creation. As the "way," wisdom is the blueprint providing the codes for creating the various domains of creation. The design precedes the act of creation; the way precedes the works of the Creator.

The personification of this "way" indicates that wisdom has a dynamic personal relationship with God. Wisdom inspires and informs God in the creation process. For God to "acquire" this way at the very beginning is to recognise God as the supreme Sage. It is this Sage that employs wisdom as the means of creating the cosmos.

> YHWH by wisdom founded Earth
> and by understanding established the skies
> (Proverbs 3:19).

It is not insignificant that the closing announcement of wisdom is one of celebration. Wisdom rejoices in creation and with humanity. The living design that integrates the codes of the cosmos is not viewed as a passive, lifeless blueprint, but a vibrant, living, driving presence. The mystery called wisdom at the core of the cosmos is a voice inviting all who would be wise to explore her facets, discover her presence, and celebrate her codes.

Ultimately then, wisdom is viewed as having a special personal relationship with God. She is seen as a living force that, from the very beginning, guides God in the creation of the various domains of the cosmos and the establishment of their respective codes.

Wisdom in my tradition

The preceding discussion of the several dimensions of wisdom in nature according to the Hebrew Scriptures highlights a rich tradition of mystery and spirituality associated with wisdom, a tradition that might well have motivated my community to explore our deep connections with nature.

Upon reflection, I now realise that any suggestion of wisdom as a mystery in nature or as a spiritual force in the universe was not so much suppressed as totally ignored by mainline Christian traditions.

Wisdom in my tradition was first of all understood as a unique attribute of God, the capacity of the omniscient One to choose, dispose, and direct the proper means to the proper ends (Job 12:13; Isaiah 55:8–9). The greatest demonstration of this wisdom was the way God planned creation and salvation. Although many of the wise counsels of God have been revealed to us, God, in God's wisdom, kept many mysteries hidden.

Human wisdom was viewed simply as the proper application of the truths about creation and salvation revealed to us through the Scriptures. Nature was not recognised as a source of wisdom that was relevant spiritually. One did not read nature to acquire wisdom. Or as Katharine Dell explains, "Wisdom has been regarded as very much life from the human side in contrast to divine revelation... with a pragmatism that is firmly grounded in concern for human beings" (2010, 56).

The wisdom figure in Proverbs 8 was read in my tradition as a poetic personification of the wisdom of God, not as a living blueprint in nature. Or this figure of wisdom was interpreted as an Old Testament anticipation of the *logos/Word* in John 1, the second person of the Trinity at work with the Father in the creation of the world.

Wisdom was never taken seriously as a deep dimension of nature and a mystery to be explored. As for the search for wisdom by God the Sage in Job 28, that text was viewed as pure poetry and not to be integrated into our spiritual lives.

Wisdom in nature

In addition to the inbuilt genetic code that governs how a creature lives, moves, and reproduces, there are numerous examples of how living beings can make wise decisions that enable them to survive. This inner capacity or code, which can be identified as a wisdom impulse, may lead a community to take a path that has not been part of their previous experience. I cite two examples: elephants in Rwanda, and fairy penguins in South Africa.

In Rwanda, the decade of development projects (1973–83) was launched by a dictatorial military regime that frequently violated the Earth. For example, officers from the army and relatives of the dictator began cutting down the natural forest of Gishwati in order to sell the timber and get rich quickly. In the forest lived people from the Impunyu tribe (who were given the derogatory name of "pygmy" by colonial invaders). The Impunyu, who are the poorest people of the land, lived in harmony with the creatures of the forest. The forest was their common home; forest wisdom guided survival.

As the forest was cleared, the Impunyi and the monkeys lost their sources of food and began to move to another forest. Their forest, they said, had been contaminated. One day, in sympathy, all the elephants of that forest also left in one mass exodus to a forest in a neighbouring country. They knew their home had been violated and they had become victims of "development." Moved by an inner wisdom, an impulse to survive, they went into exile in solidarity with their forest community, and never returned.

A few years ago, there was a massive oil spill off the coast of South Africa. Gradually the oil moved towards Robin Island (near Capetown), home for a large colony of fairy penguins. A group of individuals rescued hundreds of penguins from the island and relocated them to the eastern side of the cape, about a thousand miles away. They tagged three of the penguins to see what would happen.

After some weeks, when most of the oil spill had been cleaned up, the fairy penguins began to return home. An inner wisdom guided them. Not only did they swim the thousand miles home, they also took a detour south at one point to avoid swimming though a shark-infested area. With their return we hear their voice: this is our place on the planet no matter where you try to relocate us. Respect us and our home!

These dramatic examples direct us to appreciate that innate wisdom is true of every living creature, and indeed of every domain of our living planet. The wisdom of the ant community, matched throughout nature, should not be dismissed as mere "instinct."

Following the lead of scientists, we become aware that such inner codes are also found in cells, genes, and molecules. Scientists speak of "information" imbedded in nature. Even atoms have a mysterious inner ability/information that enables them to organise themselves into molecules, which in turn combine and evolve into biological life forms and complex ecosystems. Nature, it seems, has an inherent blueprint that activates and orders her laws, forces, and systems. That blueprint is appropriately identified as wisdom.

Some are ready to speak of a "selfish gene" as the driving force in evolution. Why not explore instead the presence of a wisdom code in genes and the rest of nature. For as Sanguin says,

> It is disingenuous to simply say that a "selfish gene" is responsible for this ordering. What gives genetic material the intelligence to wind itself up to more complex forms? Why would mind emerge from mindless matter? From whence this mysterious dance between chaos and order that results in conscious beings who can ask questions about it? (2007, 235)

In his interpretation of the priceless treasure in Matthew 13:44–45, Sanguin argues that argues that Jesus, as Wisdom's child (Matthew 11:19), reveals the way to wisdom.

He maintains that

> the kin-dom of God is the spiritual awareness that
> Sophia/Wisdom is the hidden wholeness, the very
> presence of the divine, at work and at play in the
> heart of all creation. The path of humility reveals
> her presence everywhere and in everything. The uni-
> verse and the planet earth are infused with her glori-
> ous presence making all things whole, for those who
> have eyes to see and ears to hear... The beginning of
> wisdom is the awareness that the whole living Earth
> is a divine manifestation of Sophia (2007, 174).

For some like Sanguin, an awareness of Wisdom/Sophia as
a divine manifestation in nature is the appropriate point of
departure. For others, the very code in every component
of creation is a dimension of wisdom; the information, the
blueprint, the mystery that guides evolution and creation of
ecosystems in nature.

Assuming the above understanding of wisdom as a divine
manifestation in nature is relevant in an age when we speak of
genetic codes, habitats, and interdependent ecosystems, what
does wisdom mean as we face colliding codes in a changing climate? How do we redress the balance? James Lovelock
responds by claiming that Earth herself will cry aloud and
take revenge on humanity. He claims that "global heating" is
pushing us to the brink of destruction. "We live in a planet,"
he claims, "that can respond to the changes we make either by
cancelling the changes or cancelling us" (Lovelock 2006, 3).

The issues before us in this context are how wisdom will respond, and just as importantly, how we will respond.

Some may well compare my analysis with the deep ecology of Arne Naess and others. In spite of titles like *The Ecology of Wisdom*, there are relatively few connections made with the wisdom tradition that I have outlined above. Works on deep ecology are relevant to the question of mystery at the heart of the planet, but they rarely explore the mystery of wisdom as a deep dimension of nature.

Wisdom in my world

The worldview of ecology and the challenge of ancient biblical texts have led me to reinterpret many of my experiences, whether they be daily encounters with nature or memorable moments at special locations.

On one memorable occasion, I sat on the shore of a bay in Auckland, New Zealand. Around me hundreds of bar-tailed godwits had gathered from points all around the island. All day they raced round in a frenzy of feeding. Suddenly, as if a signal were given and received from within each of them, they all began to circle and form a spiral of spinning life. Slowly the spiral swirled out to sea, and the godwits were on their way to Alaska to feed, breed, and nurture.

Flight Wisdom

At that moment
I could sense Wisdom.
The wisdom of flight
and the wisdom of memory
encoded in their spirit.
I was conscious of the amazing intelligence
of fellow Earth beings
guiding themselves non-stop
across the ocean to a place
more than ten thousand kilometres away!

And I was humbled.

While standing on my balcony watching a violent thunderstorm roll in across the ocean towards my home, the biblical passage about God discerning dimensions of wisdom in the weather came to life for me. God found wisdom in the force of the wind; the wind I felt knew the weight needed to drive the storm onto the land. God found wisdom in the volume of the waters; the clouds I watched knew how much water to carry and splash onto the land. God found wisdom in the rule of the rain; the rain I saw coming knew how to fall at the times and on the places needed. In sum, God found wisdom in the "way" of the thunderstorm, the inner code that guides all dimensions of the climate ecosystem. And I could sense that wisdom spelled out across the sky before me.

Another time, a more mundane encounter with a hive of ants and the memory of a passage from Proverbs provoked a similar reaction.

Earth Wisdom

If wisdom is the knowledge
handed down from the past
regarding the best ways
to live and move and have our being,
then Earth is a treasury of wisdom.

An old proverb says
"Consider the ways of the ant and be wise!"
For years I read that adage
as advice on how I as a human
might become wise by watching an ant.

Now I realise the ant too has wisdom
and knows from its ancestors
how to find food, store food,
and communicate with its kin
while travelling to and from its storehouse.

Wisdom is stored in seeds
that know how to germinate,
to reach out to the sun,
to flower and to spread seeds
imbedded with the same wisdom.

Wisdom extends
to all domains of Earth,
from the highest mountain
to the deepest ocean,
from the brains of a blind bat
to the genes of a jellyfish.

All the genes that have evolved on Earth
are imbedded with codes
of information,
wisdom at the deepest level,
the impulse to know how to live
and not just be.

I now know
Earth is filled with wisdom
worth knowing.

Sustaining the mystery of wisdom

Earth's ecosystems are indeed guided by an innate wisdom and we are called to discern the parameters of that wisdom and strive to maintain the balance of nature.

The follies of humanity are apparent. Humans have been bent on dominating the many domains of nature, especially arable land, forests, and rivers. The domains of nature are viewed as God-given resources to exploit at will. The resulting environmental catastrophes are evidence of our folly.

Especially significant is the breaking of domain boundaries. According to the wise, the scientists of old, each domain has its "place," and the elements of each domain have their "place" or locus in nature (Job 28). Humans, however, have extracted fossil fuels from their "place" in the domains below Earth where they belong, transformed them into various gaseous forms and disseminated them in another domain; namely, the atmosphere. The result is an atmosphere overloaded with greenhouse gases and a disruption of the existing balance of the "ways" or laws of nature.

We now face unstable climate patterns. The previous codes or ways that governed the cycles and patterns of the winds, seas, storms, and droughts have been disrupted. The laws that governed the weather patterns no longer prevail.

Let me use the example of the 2009 bushfires in the State of Victoria in Australia. As a boy on the farm, I knew the way of bushfires. I knew the force of the hot north wind. I knew the speed of the fire, and the time needed to prepare to escape the flames. I knew how to burn firebreaks to retard the fire. But with climate change, all of these factors changed. On Black Saturday, all the known patterns of a bushfire were transcended.

With climate change has come increased hot spells and decreased rainfall. The rise of carbon dioxide in the atmosphere has led to increased vegetation in the region, much of which was tinder dry on Black Saturday. The Black Saturday bushfire was hotter, faster, and stronger than any classic bushfire. The way of the bushfire we once knew has been transformed.

There are other examples. The way of the seemingly eternal ice caps has changed and seas are rising. The ways of the storm, the drought, and the floods have changed. The way of the ocean is changing as villages, like those on the shores of Orissa on the Bay of Bengal, are inundated by incoming waters. With these changes in the codes of our climate, how do we interpret our cosmos? Where do we find wisdom? How do we find a way to sustain wisdom in nature and maintain the balance needed for a healthy planet?

The Covenant

Perhaps we might again accept the invitation to covenant with Earth and work with our planet as a partner. Our commitment might be articulated as follows.

Given the mystery that many of the "ways" of wisdom imbedded by God in creation (Job 28:23–27) have been disturbed by human greed and folly, we are invited to discern wisdom in nature, sustain the balance of nature, and prepare for the impending difficulties resulting from climate change.

Conclusion

Wisdom in nature is another mystery that I have encountered, whether through exploring the insights of ecology or facing the forces of an oncoming thunderstorm; whether through probing deep ecology or intensely observing the way of the ant.

I would probably not have been so alert to this mystery had it not been for the challenge of biblical texts such as Job 28, where God is portrayed as Sage in search of wisdom, a mystery that God locates in the very forces of the weather. Wisdom is not an attribute of God, but a sacred dimension encoded in the forces of nature.

Obviously, one does not need to take this poem literally, but we should recognise how the wise of old were in tune with nature and that their discernment went far beyond the mechanical laws governing creation. They recognised wisdom as an innate spiritual-cum-physical dimension of nature. Such insight deserves to be celebrated and explored anew.

Can this amazing mystery called wisdom that impinges on every aspect of life on Earth be designated a sacrament, a vehicle for imparting life and healing through the domains of nature? If we recognise wisdom as more than a physical force in nature, we may well celebrate wisdom as a blessing that mediates the sacred.

Whatever wisdom I may discern in nature, wisdom persists as a mystery, a spiritual response. And so I ask whether wisdom is not another way in which Presence in creation reveals itself to me. If Presence permeates the planet, then surely one way in which Presence is apparent is in the wisdom innate in the ecosystems of our planet and in the blueprint encoded in our cosmos. And so I invite you to worship with me by exploring the wisdom in nature.

Blessing

May the ways of wisdom,
imbedded in the codes and laws of nature,
confront our consciousness
so that we recognize, celebrate, and sustain
the mystery of the blueprint that sustains us
and informs the incredible impulses
deep within the ecosystems of our planet.

Chapter Seven

The Mystery of Compassion

A Violet Mystery

Earth is filled with
the compassion of the Lord.
(Psalm 33:5)

Compassion

Compassion is the impulse to share the suffering of another so as to care for, comfort, or heal the other. Those who have a burning compassion deep inside are said to have soul. This chapter explores how compassion may be expressed as a spiritual force in the wider context of nature.

We investigated the mystery of presence and discovered how one part of nature may be present to another part. But are they present *for* each other, supportive and empathetic of the other's reality? Is compassion another mystery in nature?

We explored the life impulse in nature, the inner force that drives components of the cosmos to evolve, live, and interact. But do such life impulses also include the capacity to go beyond individual survival-of-the-fittest to sustaining and healing others through compassion or interrelationship?

We discovered voices emanating from nature that we have not bothered to heed in the past. Do those voices reflect more than expressions of lament and praise? Do the cries from nature also include expressions of care, concern, and empathy?

We explored the mystery of wisdom imbedded in natural laws, systems, and relationships. Does this wisdom go beyond the processes of ordering and designing the elements of nature to include compassion for its components?

In exploring this possibility of compassion in nature, we could start by asking whether the cosmos has soul. The question is not whether creation has a soul, but whether the cosmos has an inner dimension that knows pain, passion, mystery, communion, and life. And if the cosmos does indeed have soul, how might I connect with this deep spiritual dimension of the universe? How might soul manifest?

We associate this deep passion with the colour violet in the rainbow of mysteries.

Compassion in the Scriptures

One of the classic texts quoted in times of pain and despair is Psalm 23. At first glance, this Psalm affirms the concern of a compassionate God, who is portrayed as a shepherd ready to meet all the needs of his flock. This well-known Psalm begins,

The Lord is my shepherd,
I shall not want.
He makes me lie down in green pastures;
he leads me beside still waters;
he restores my soul.

If we look closely at the imagery of the text, however, we recognise that there are dimensions to the compassion that relate to our question about compassion in nature. How might soul be manifest?

The psalmist is not concerned merely with his physical needs. His *nephesh*, his total self, is in need of healing. He needs to be brought back to the fullness of life.

The compassionate shepherd does not heal this sufferer with a simple snap of the fingers. Rather, he uses a connection with nature to facilitate the healing. He takes the sufferer to green pastures so he can "lie down" and find peace. He leads the sufferer to still waters, to a calming place where he can find new strength. The shepherd's goal is to "restore" the sufferer's psyche (*nephesh* in Hebrew).

The imagery of God being "with" and showing "comfort" is a clear expression of compassion. It may appear to the sufferer that he or she is "going through hell," the valley of the shadow of death. Still, he/she has the assurance that no matter what the location, God will be compassionate.

God's compassion may also be associated with the term *chesed*. This Hebrew word is often rendered as "loving-kindness," but since it is regularly associated with the covenant, it may be better translated as "covenant concern" or "compassion." In Psalm 33, in the context of God creating the skies by the divine word and the stars by divine breath, the Psalmist proclaims,

He loves righteousness and justice;
Earth is filled with the *chesed* of the Lord (33:5).

Earlier we celebrated the radiant presence of God filling Earth. Now we discover that, according to this Psalm, not only does God's presence permeate this planet but God's covenant compassion also fills it. In contemporary terms, we may say Earth has soul.

The dilemma we face when reading the Old Testament Scriptures, however, is that so many events relating to nature seem to lack expressions of God's compassion. In the biblical story of the Flood, for example, the narrative seems to commence with an expression of divine compassion. God's heart grieves because of the sinfulness of humans (Genesis 6:5–8). The flood sent as divine judgment, however, does not seem to reflect a further sense of compassion. Noah finds grace and rescues representative creatures. But all other life on Earth is destroyed. Where is the compassion in such an action? What have these creatures done to deserve such cruel treatment? Or, as I explain in a recent work of mine, this biblical text is "grey" and not "green," cruel and not compassionate" (2009, 12–13):

Whatever the Old Testament may have understood about the nature of God as both judge and deliverer, the New Testament portrait of Jesus is believed to be a reflection of the compassionate love of God. Jesus heals lepers of their leprosy, restores the sight of the blind, and expels the unclean spirits from the possessed. He identifies with the unclean, the outcast, and the non-Israelite. He is a man of compassion for those in society who are excluded.

In the New Testament, the compassion of Jesus extends to the human community of his day rather than to nature. Admittedly, after his temptation, Jesus joins the wild beasts in the wilderness, notices the lilies of the field, and uses mud to heal the blind man; but rarely does he relate his message directly to nature. Jesus does not explore whether the cosmos has soul. Yet when he is crucified, the natural world responds with agony and empathy.

The Spiritual Experience of a Centurion

We had crucified Jesus,
hung him high on the cross to die,
listened to the mockery of the crowd
and the scorn of the robbers.
Then I became aware of the compassion of creation.
For three hours the skies mourned,
covering the land with darkness.
The Earth began to quake,
convulse in sympathy as graves burst open
and the dead were disturbed.
In the temple, the veil covering God's presence
was torn apart
and the very presence of God was in pain.
I too felt the pain and the pathos
as Earth quaked.
And my spirit erupted,
"This Jesus was the Son of God!"

Compassion in my tradition

In my tradition, we said that Jesus' suffering on the cross for us was the ultimate expression of God's compassion. We even went so far as to say that since Jesus was God, we could speak of God crucified and God suffering for us because of our sins. The cross was the epitome of God's compassion.

The Eucharist was one special occasion when we were able to partake of the body and blood of Jesus Christ and thereby taste, as it were, the compassion, love, and healing power of God via a sacrament. At the Table of the Lord, the members of the family of God were said to experience a glimpse of heaven, far from the trials and tribulations of life on Earth.

This sense of compassion through the Eucharist was very meaningful to me in times of trial. This compassion, however, was understood to be an expression of God's love for God's people. We heard of no corresponding divine compassion for creation, no message that Christ also suffered for and with nature.

More recently, Christian scholars have reflected on texts from Ephesians 2 and Colossians 1 to recognise the concept of the cosmic Christ. Denis Edwards, for example, argues in the light of such passages that Christ is the very image of God, the first born through whom all things are created. Christ is the very Wisdom of God incarnate (1995, 35).

Through this incarnate One, the saving plan of God extends to include "gathering all things up in Christ, things in heaven and in Earth" (Ephesians 1:10). "All things" in this and related texts, refers to all God's created worlds, not just humans. Even more significant perhaps is the text of Colossians where it is said,

> For in him all the fullness of God was pleased to
>   dwell,
> and through him God was pleased to reconcile to
> himself all things.
> whether on Earth or in heaven,
> by making peace through the blood of the cross
> (Colossians 1:19–20).

The risen Christ is understood to be a power at work in the cosmos that will, in some way, effect reconciliation between God and creation, a feat achieved because of "the blood of the cross." In short, the cosmic Christ seems to be identified as a compassionate power alive in the universe.

These passages, however, tended to have little influence on how we related to nature, to this temporary abode called planet Earth. Any image of reconciliation, peace, and renewal of creation was relegated to the end of time, to the termination of this cosmos. Any suggestion that Mother Earth may have soul was rejected.

After all, as the final verse of the hymn *Jesus Loves Me* announces, the ultimate goal of Jesus' compassion is to "take me home on high"!

Compassion in nature

When we explore the cosmos we tend to be aware of numerous massive forces at work. Pivotal among all those forces is gravity. Unseen, it controls movements of solar systems and galaxies, the rotation of Earth around the sun, and the spinning of stars through space. It is gravity that keeps our feet on the ground.

Compassion at first does not seem to belong among the forces that operate across the cosmos. In the timeline of evolution, compassion and nurturing tend to be regarded as but recent tendencies in human consciousness. Yet we may also consider whether, since compassion has now evolved as an important factor in life on Earth, it is an inherent dimension of our expanding cosmos.

The possibility that humans are the only ones conscious of compassion at the current moment in the evolutionary process, however, does not negate the possibility of its presence, latent or otherwise, in prior stages of evolution.

From an ecological perspective, I would argue there is an impulse in Earth that is more than biological, yet found at the very centre of all that lives – the impulse of the spirit to nurture, and thereby show compassion. Giving birth is itself an act of nurture through which Earth sustains and bonds with life. The process of nurture extends to all aspects of life on Earth and indeed to Earth itself. And that impulse, it can be argued, is from the compassionate Spirit at the centre, with whom all things are connected.

Suzuki and Amanda McConnell call this spiritual impulse of Earth to nurture the "law of love" in nature. Humans are all too ready to view themselves as the one species that knows how to nurture or love. Listen again to the insights of Suzuki and McConnell.

> When we observe the care with which a mud dauber prepares a mud enclosure, inserts a paralysed victim as food and deposits an egg, can we be so anthropocentric as to deny this the name of love. How else can we interpret the male sea horse's protective act of accepting babies into his pouch, the months-long incubation of an emperor penguin's egg on the feet of its vigilant parent, or the epic journey of Pacific salmon returning from their natal stream to mate and die in the creation of the next generation? If these are innate actions dictated by genetically encoded instructions, all the more reason to conclude that love in its many manifestations is fashioned into the very blueprint of life (1997, 173).

In discussing the generally held belief that intense competition is evolution's driving force, and that any semblance of love for our fellow human beings results only from God's good grace, Tim Flannery cites Darwin's claim that it is "the content face of nature" that reigns most of the time. As Flannery says,

From the love that sustains the family to the beetle that writes on the tree, every bit stems from evolution by natural selection. If competition is evolution's natural force, then the cooperative world is its legacy. And legacies are important, for they can endure long after the force that created them ceases to be (2010, 31).

Healing is also a dynamic dimension of nature and a vital expression of compassion. We can discern healing in everything from the way injured animals care for each other to the way denuded landscapes are restored by the wind carrying seeds, by the soil that renews fertility, and by the rain that activates life. The forces of nature share in the healing process to facilitate survival. As David Suzuki writes,

> It is a mistake to compare living systems to machines. Mechanical devices constantly wear out with time unless they are carefully maintained and repaired by people. Living things persist on their own, healing, replacing, adapting, and reproducing in order to continue. If the total of all life on earth is a super-organism, then it must have processes that perpetuate its survival (1997, 154).

So it seems that compassion, whether understood as cooperation and caring, or empathy and nurture, is integral to the nature of our living planet. But is it a spiritual force that evolves from the distant past and reaches deep into the cosmos? And could such a spiritual force be named God?

Compassion in my world

I now explore the most profound of all the mysteries in nature. Is there indeed compassion in the cosmos? Does my mother, Earth, have soul? Is there is a spiritual force in nature that is passionate, compassionate, and caring (God)?

Many scientists find it difficult to discern empathy in nature. In an interview on November 3, 2011, Stephen Frye argued that "it all boils down to sex and food." His take is that evolution is ultimately a battle to survive by hunting for food and reproducing one's genes. Frye seems to find no compassion in nature, only competition.

So is there compassion in nature? Where might I discern, feel, or know Earth's soul?

In short, do the mysteries I have explored and experienced enable me to discern compassion in the cosmos, or at least in this planet? Or is this the ultimate mystery I must simply take on faith?

On a personal level, I feel deep compassion for the "stolen generation," Aboriginal people who were abducted by officials and dumped in so-called orphanages in accordance with the policy to keep Australia white (Habel, 1999). I feel the trauma of Dalit (untouchable) women in the mountains of South India, and taste the pain of people who have suffered abuse because of their beliefs. However, I am forced to another level of discernment and consciousness when challenged to experience soul in Mother Earth or explore compassion in the cosmos.

In the aftermath of the 2004 tsunamis, I came to appreciate that not only humans experienced caring and compassion during these events. I sensed, whether in faith or otherwise, that planet Earth was also groaning empathetically.

Earth Compassion

Many who explore the evolution
of my mother Earth
tend to see a battleground,
the survival of the fiercest in
a dog-eat-dog world.

My sympathy
is with those new scientists
who discern the survival of the caring,
the web of compassion
that creates community
and integrates ecosystems.
Can I trust their views?

And Earth, some would argue,
is part of that community
communicating concern
from species to species
and from the depths to the heights.
Can I discern such a mystery?

Then one frightening day,
I sensed something in the tsunami
that flooded islands of the Pacific
and inundated Indian Ocean shores.

The groaning of Earth,
the dangerous dislocations,
were not just selfish quaking
but a message of empathy to all creatures,
a caring cry
that some Earth beings heard
and then left for higher ground,
like the elephants in Sri Lanka
and the reptiles of Acer.

Sad to say,
most of the Earth beings called humans
were not listening
and so did not sense Earth's compassion.

This ultimate mystery challenges me to reflect on my own memories about a crucified God.

I remember the amazing claim at the beginning of John's gospel that a dimension of God called the *logos*, which was understood in the ancient Greek world as word/reason/intellect, was a force involved in the origins of creation. This force can be compared with the mystery of Wisdom explored in the previous chapter.

Even more amazing is the claim that this *logos* became "flesh," and so part of the natural world. In the light of this radical union we can say that mind becomes matter, body possesses soul, and the spiritual knows the nature of the material. In other words, there is ultimately a oneness of God with nature. This suggests that God knows how to empathise with nature.

However we may understand the nature of God, I have a sense that God did not remain detached in determining the course of the cosmos, but became a compassionate force that is in, with, and under the very stuff of nature. In my exploration of the mystery of compassion, these memories intensified my consciousness and my ecological awareness and allowed me to discern compassion as a deep spiritual force in the cosmos.

This new consciousness enables me to sense more than Presence, Wisdom, and Wonder in the nature that embraces me. I also sense Compassion sustaining this planet and surging through the entire cosmos.

Sustaining the mystery

In the face of natural disasters, one tends to feel compassion first and foremost for the human beings. But it is hard to ignore the blue wrens and array of other birds destroyed by the massive bushfires in Victoria in 2010, or the wild animals drowned by extensive flooding in Asia. Yet, our first concern is generally for our fellow human beings.

The Covenant

The focus of this mystery of compassion, however, is not solely on a human expression of sympathy for Earth beings. Our goal is to become aware of the compassion of the cosmos, to explore whether Earth has soul and how we might be partners with Earth in showing empathy for domains of Earth in pain. We are invited to participate in more than raising consciousness about the crises of our planet.

> Given the mystery that there is compassion in the cosmos and that Mother Earth has soul, we are invited to discover compassion in nature (Psalm 33:4–7) and to explore how we might express faith in that compassion by being a partner of Earth in healing creation.

Where then do I sense compassion around me as a mystery, a genuinely spiritual dimension of the cosmos? Where do I have a sense of sharing a passion that is more than human-to-human? Where in the wider world, the cosmos I know and celebrate, do I experience the kind of soul I know from my life with singing and suffering humans?

As I walk into woods at sunset I become aware that all around me are sharing the moment with me. We share each other's presence; we present ourselves to each other. Beyond we share the sunset. And beyond the sunset we share the Presence that permeates our planet and makes us conscious of presence. Can I also discern a dimension of compassion in the Presence that impinges on my consciousness?

When I take a lump of clay in my hands and reflect on my origin as an Earth being, I realise I share a common origin with the fauna and flora around me. We have a common mother. We share Earth's soil, her nurture, her life, her pains. Can I also sense my mother's love? Does she have soul? Can I discover the mystery of compassion in my mother?

If I contemplate the wonders of a mountain or a ravine, I become aware that I am not alone. Wondering is shared by all around me. And the very wonders that leave me awe-struck also express wonder and point to a mystery we seek to know, the Wonder of all wonders. Wonder is everywhere, but is the mystery of soul also found in wonder? Is Wonder connected with cosmic compassion?

At times I am acutely conscious of being alive, passionate about the breathing, wondering, and feeling I share with others. I am not alone; I share that passion with every being around me. I share in a web of life that connects with a mystery of deep beginnings and future connections, with the agonies of evolution and the hopes of the future. Can I feel within that very Impulse that stirs in the life I know a deep compassion, the mystery of empathetic life emerging throughout this cosmos?

At other times I share the pains of my planet, the agonies of my mother. I am acutely aware of the suffering caused by environmental crises, past and present. As I walk this planet I am learning to empathise with the voices of Earth emerging from the landscape, as my Indigenous brothers and sisters have long done. But when I visit scorched Earth sites on this planet, they are screaming to be heard and healed. Are they selfish cries or do they also express compassion, a mystery I seek to share?

An extraordinary experience happens for me when I pause, like the wise of old, to discern the mystery of wisdom embedded in the very fabric of nature. I share wisdom with every ant who knows within how to be an ant, to share life and death with other ants, and to impart its wisdom to me if I know how to discern the way of an ant. Wisdom is the blueprint in each of us; do we then also have capacity for grasping empathy in wisdom? And is the Wisdom that masterminds all ecosystems also encoded with compassion?

Finally, I face my rainbow formed of mysteries that reach deep into the origins of the cosmos and I search for that compassion – the passion I share with nature. That compassion is deeper than me, than my level of consciousness, than my limited spirituality. Compassion means sharing my passion as an Earth being for sensing Presence, discerning Wisdom, hearing the Voice of Earth, feeling the pulse of Life, being awestruck by Wonder, and discerning the mystery in it all as a spiritual force we may name as Compassion or God.

Blessing

May the compassion of the cosmos,
and the empathy of Earth,
stir within you a consciousness
of a spiritual force in nature
that shares pain,
heals hearts,
and nurtures hope.

Conclusion
Rainbow Blessings

In this book I have sought to explore the spiritual dimensions of nature, and to capture something of the joy that finding these mysteries in nature brings to me, despite my very traditional Lutheran heritage. My intention was not to develop a new eco-theology that somehow incorporated the insights of my adventures. Nor was I interested in trying to establish a new template for Earth spirituality.

I wrote this book as an invitation, given the new worldview of ecology and the current environmental crisis, to explore a rainbow of mysteries in nature, to celebrate the mysteries as sacred dimensions of my world, and to be involved in sustaining them.

I offer the following blessings.

Red – Radiant Presence

I invite you to share the following blessing, rich and red and radiant.

> May your evolving consciousness quiver
> when you sense the mystery
> of Presence permeating our planet.

Orange – The Clay of Earth

I invite you to share the following blessing with your kin.

> May your whole being come alive
> when you feel the mystery of Mother Earth
> birthing you and all fellow Earth beings.

Gold – The Wonder of the Wild

I invite you to share the following blessing with the domains of the wild.

> May you celebrate
> when you experience the mystery
> of Wonder overwhelming you with wonder.

Green – The Pulse of Life

I invite you to share the following blessing as you feel the pulse of Earth.

May your spirit sing
when you feel the mystery of Life
pulsing throughout our planet.

Blue – The Voice from the Deep

I invite you to share the following blessing as you listen to Mother Earth.

May your inner ear
hear the cries of Mother Earth,
and may you respond with empathy.

Indigo – The Wisdom in Nature

I invite you to share the following blessing with nature.

May your enquiring mind explode
when you discover the mystery of Wisdom
encoded in the blueprints of nature.

Purple – Cosmic Compassion

I invite you to share the following blessing as an expression
of your faith in the ultimate mystery of the cosmos.

When you explore the mystery
of Compassion permeating the universe
may you discover that the cosmos has soul.

Appendix 1

Sharing Earth Spirituality and Earth Mission

Workshop Suggestions

Introduction

The materials outlined in this book are also designed to support workshops for participants who wish to explore Earth spirituality in tandem with worship and meditation, or as motivation for Earth mission. Each chapter of the book contains material appropriate for discussion, meditation, reflection, and forward planning.

It is ideal if workshop participants have the opportunity to interact and connect directly with the worlds and pulses of nature, so the introductions to the various rites suggest suitable locations (see Appendix 2). The locations can be varied to suit the needs and circumstances of particular workshops at diverse times of the year.

Sequence

The book's seven chapters and the seven rites in Appendix 2 have been organised as a three-day workshop as follows. This sequence may, of course, be varied to accommodate the needs or circumstances of those involved.

Friday Afternoon	Introduction to the Workshop
Friday Evening	Mystery of Presence – Chapter 1 Sacred site at sunset
Saturday Morning	Mystery of Being Earth-Born – Chapter 2 Sacred site on home ground
Saturday Afternoon	Mystery of Wonder – Chapter 3 Sacred site on the rocks
Saturday Evening	Mystery of Life – Chapter 4 Sacred site in a forest
Sunday Morning	Mystery of Voice – Chapter 5 Scorched Earth sites
Sunday Afternoon	Mystery of Wisdom – Chapter 6 Sacred site in the garden
Sunday Evening	Mystery of Compassion – Chapter 7 Sacred site in the wild Closing of Workshop

Workshop Program

The common structure of each chapter provides a pattern for participants to follow as a group or with the aid of a mentor/facilitator. I have generally divided each chapter/workshop segment into three parts with appropriate questions for discussion, meditation, and planning. This structure is signalled in the Introduction where the five steps of analysis and reflection are identified. Typical questions for discussion are offered as a stimulus for participation in the workshop. Each chapter/segment of the workshop would incorporate the three parts below.

Part One

1. Exploring the Mystery in the Bible

- Do you resonate with the biblical texts cited in the relevant chapter relating to the mystery being explored? If so, how?
- Are there other texts, biblical or otherwise, that help you appreciate this mystery in nature?

2. The Mystery in Your Tradition

- How does/did your religious community understand the mystery being explored? Is/was it suppressed or ignored as a dimension of nature, or is/was it celebrated? If so, how?

Part Two

3. Exploring the Mystery in Nature

- Have the sciences of ecology and/or evolution re-oriented your thinking and understanding about this mystery in nature?
- Has the environmental crisis played a role in changing your attitude to nature? Has it led you to connect more closely with this mystery in nature?

4. Exploring the Mystery in Your Personal World

- Describe a personal experience where this mystery in nature came alive for you. How did you react? How did others react?

- Did your experience of this mystery in nature change your understanding of God or the divine?

Part Three

5. A Mission to Sustain

- What kind of exercises, activities, worship, or meditation might help you sustain a sense of this mystery in your faith and life?
- Does a deeper understanding of this mystery in nature also mean a mission call to hear the cries of Earth and be involved in the work of caring for Earth?

Celebrating the Mystery

The sacred rite at a sacred site may be held for each mystery as a way of further celebrating the mystery explored in that session.

Workshop Opening and Closing

Participants may wish to use the following litany at the commencement of a workshop.

LEADER   We come to this moment,
at this sacred place in the universe
to focus our consciousness on
the mysteries of our cosmos.

PEOPLE   **On the mystery of Presence
that permeates our planet.**

LEADER   On the mystery of the identity
we share with fellow Earth beings.

PEOPLE   **On the mystery of Wonder
that evokes wonder within us.**

LEADER   On the mystery of Life
pulsing through our planet.

PEOPLE   **On the mystery of the Voice
of Earth we hear groaning below.**

LEADER   On the mystery of Wisdom
implanted in all of nature.

PEOPLE   **On the mystery of Compassion
that sustains our cosmos.**

LEADER   We focus our consciousness
PEOPLE   **on the mysteries of our cosmos.**

The workshop may close using the *Rainbow Blessing* found in the Conclusion of this book, a blessing that participants may share with each other.

Appendix 2

Seven Rites at Seven Sites

Exploring Mystery in Nature

The seven rites included in this appendix correspond to the seven chapters of the book. These rites may be celebrated as part of a workshop or for individual moments of reflection, meditation, and worship. They may also be included within the various liturgies during *The Season of Creation* (www.seasonofcreation.com) or other occasions celebrating creation.

The central symbol used in these rites is an ***Earth bowl***. The Earth bowl is a large, relatively flat terracotta bowl or pot that contains fresh earth, preferably orange in colour. At key points in the rites, participants focus on the Earth bowl as a symbol of Earth and perform symbolic actions relating to the relevant mystery. In each of the rites, a symbol of that mystery is planted in the Earth bowl in some way. The symbols may be actual items or pictures (for example, bird or ant nest) or other items that work for you in the context of the mystery.

Each rite may also have a wider setting in nature that is appropriate to the theme, whether sitting on a hillside watching a sunset, standing on rocks looking out to sea, or meditating by a river in a forest. Participants may be in the physical setting or in the imagination of their consciousness.

Rite One	Sacred site at sunset — The Mystery of Presence
	A glass of red wine — a symbol of Presence
Rite Two	Sacred site on home ground — The Mystery of Being Earth-Born
	Orange soil in the Earth bowl — a symbol of being an Earth being
Rite Three	Sacred site on the rocks — The Mystery of Wonder
	A rock embracing a fossil — a symbol of Wonder
Rite Four	Sacred site in a forest — The Mystery of Life
	Eucalyptus and rosemary — symbols of Life
Rite Five	Scorched Earth sites — The Mystery of Voice
	Burnt branch, dead coral — symbols of scorched domains
Rite Six	Sacred site in a garden — The Mystery of Wisdom
	A replica of an ant's nest in the Earth bowl — symbol of encoded Wisdom
Rite Seven	Sacred site in the wild — The Mystery of Compassion
	A replica of a bird's nest and eggs — symbol of Compassion and caring

A Sacred Site at Sunset

The Mystery of Presence

The Setting

Participants gather round the ***Earth bowl.*** A glass of red wine, a symbol of Presence, stands upright in the soil. Reflect on the mystery of Presence.

And/Or

Participants gather, whether in physical space or in the imagination of their consciousness, on a hillside looking towards the west as the sun sets. The sky turns red, and they become conscious of presences and Presence surrounding them in the dusk. As the celebrant reads the script, the participants use their minds, spirits, and hearts to reflect on the words. As each line is spoken, there is an extended pause for reflection.

Discerning Presence

LEADER   Holy! Holy! Holy! The whole Earth is filled with Presence.
         (Pause.)

         The red evening light reflects Presence.
         (Pause.)

         The space beyond is penetrated with Presence.
         (Pause.)

         Landscape is alive with Presence.
         (Pause.)

         The evening air is quivering with Presence.
         (Pause.)

         The forest is pulsing with Presence.
         (Pause.)

Our planet is permeated with Presence.
(Pause.)

The ground below trembles with Presence.
(Pause.)

Our bodies are embraced by Presence.
(Pause.)

Holy! Holy! Holy! The whole Earth is filled with Presence.

Memories of Presence

LEADER   We now hear a memory of Presence as we silently reflect on the following verse.
Participants are invited to add their own memories.

Suspended in Stillness

I sat in a crevice of nature, a cove on Kangaroo Island.
It was October 3, 2009. All was still; shimmering still.
No wind or wave stirred the eerie hush,
yet there was a feeling of sheer presence, intense, close.
It was as if nature had ceased all movement
so that I might feel her pulse.
Sounds hovered in the distance.
Then the sound of silence,
of sheer stillness,
and I was suspended
in Presence.

Exploring Mystery

LEADER   We now seek to explore the mystery of Presence,
those dimensions of Presence that amaze us
and connect us with the spiritual in the world around us.

VOICE 1   Do you sense mystery in the way trees, mountains,
horizons, or seas present themselves to you?

VOICE 2   Everything that presents itself is reaching out,
inviting us to connect with nature.
That invitation is an amazing mystery,
an allurement found everywhere in nature.

VOICE 1   Do you sense mystery in the fact that every presence
connects with a prior and future Presence?

VOICE 2   Every presence we experience now connects with
prior and future Presence.
And that endless line of connected presences is a mystery deep in
the web of creation.

VOICE 1   Do you sense mystery within yourself, in the very
consciousness you have of presences?

VOICE 2   Awareness of presence flows from our consciousness,
a capacity that reveals the spiritual.
The ultimate mystery, however, is how this consciousness
is also aware of a Presence that permeates all nature,
all presences, a Presence we may call God.

Symbolic Action: Sharing Presence

LEADER   We are now invited to gather round
the Earth bowl and the glass of red wine,
a traditional symbol of Presence.

PEOPLE   **Red is the symbol of God's glory,
the Presence that permeates our planet.**

LEADER   I now take the glass of red wine
and pour it slowly across the soil in the Earth bowl
to symbolise Presence permeating our planet.

PEOPLE   **Our planet is permeated with Presence,
the vibrant Presence called God.**

LEADER   I now refill the glass with red wine
and invite you to share in the Presence
that permeates our planet.
As you share you may wish to say:
The mystery of Presence be with you.

Blessing

LEADER: I now invite you to share a blessing with each other. Face the person
next to you and repeat after me:

May the radiant Presence
filling this sanctuary called Earth
help you discover a holy of holies
shimmering red among the trees
in a location you love.

A Sacred Site on Home Ground

The Mystery of Being Earth-Born

The Setting
Participants gather round the ***Earth bowl*** that is filled with rich orange
clay/soil. The bowl symbolizes Earth as our home and our identity as
Earth beings; the orange soil symbolises the mystery of our origins.

And/Or

Participants gather, whether in physical space or in the imagination of
their consciousness, in a familiar landscape where orange rocks, a clay
bank, or rich soil can be seen and where animals run wild. As they celebrate the rite, participants reflect on the mystery of being Earth-born and
thus kin with all they see.

Returning Home to Earth

LEADER   We gather in this sacred place,
here on this sacred planet called Earth.

PEOPLE   **We gather in this sacred place
to explore the mystery of being Earth beings.**

LEADER   As we gather, we are invited to experience this time as a journey.

PEOPLE   **A spiritual journey back home to Earth.**

LEADER   We are Earth beings returning to Earth,
our home, our primal parent,
and the source of our identity.

PEOPLE	**Earth is indeed our primal parent,** **our mother, Mother Earth.**
LEADER	The invitation to return home can be heard from other Earth beings and from Earth herself. After each invitation we pause to reflect on our kinship with domains of Earth whose voices we hear.
VOICE 1	I am soil, clay, ground. I invite you to affirm our kinship. You and I are one with Earth. *(Pause.)*
VOICE 2	I am air, wind, atmosphere. I invite you to breathe and feel within the life you share with all on Earth. *(Pause.)*
VOICE 3	I am water, seas, clouds. I invite you to taste the water of life, the blessing that flows through your body. *(Pause.)*
VOICE 1	We are Earth's fauna. We too are Earth beings and we invite you to recognise your identity, as Earth being and Earth relative. *(Pause.)*
VOICE 2	We are Earth's flora, and we invite you to sing with the choirs of the forests and celebrate the joy of being an Earth being. *(Pause.)*

VOICE 3   I am Earth. I am your mother.
           And I invite you to sense deep inside
           the mystery of the moment.
           You are my child, formed in my womb,
           and born to be a free Earth being.
           Welcome home.
           (Pause.)

Earth Memories

LEADER   We now recall an Earth memory, a time when that bond with
          Mother Earth was stirred.
          You are invited to add your own memories.

An Earth Moment Memory

As I reflect on my journey
I often wonder
just where it all began.
What moment sparked my desire
to find my beginnings.

After all,
I was happy in my adoptive family,
I was a leader in my community
with my name in print
and my songs in demand.

What more could I want?

In my study of the Bible and the traditions
of my adoptive family,
I explored many approaches.
I analysed the literature,
I investigated the history,
I explored the culture.

Then ecology came onto the scene.
Just another science,
or so I thought!
Strange as it may seem,
ecology became personal.
Ecology confronted me
with a view of the world I could not ignore.
Ecology challenged my cosmology
and my faith.

Instead of being another science
that let me view nature with detachment
because I was a superior intellectual being
with a mandate to dominate creation,
ecology revealed to me who I was:
an Earth being!

Exploring Mystery

LEADER   We now seek to explore this mystery,
the mystery of being an Earth being,
the mystery of the spiritual force at our core.

VOICE 1   Do you sense mystery in the way you connect
with the very matter of Earth:
soil, microbes, and mountains?

VOICE 2   Our bodies, minds, and consciousness
evolved from Earth's matter.
To be an Earth being is to embody the spiritual.

VOICE 1   Do you sense mystery in the impulses of Earth,
the deep energies that make our Earth-being bodies
sing and celebrate?

VOICE 2   From the depths of Earth an Impulse emerges
to make you a living, singing, wondering mystery
called an Earth being.

VOICE 1   Do you sense mystery within yourself,
an awareness that as an Earth being you are spiritual?

VOICE 2   All Earth beings are spiritual,
and Earth invites us home to celebrate;
body, mind, and spirit together as one.

Symbolic Action: Sharing Earth

LEADER   You are now invited to approach the Earth bowl,
and run your hands and fingers through the soil.
There will be grains of Earth left on your hands.
(Participants run their hands through the soil in the Earth bowl.)

LEADER   You are now invited to rub your hands together
         and feel the very matter of which you are made,
         the mystery of your evolution from Earth beginnings.

PEOPLE   **We celebrate our identity!**
         We are Earth beings, born of Mother Earth.
         We celebrate our family!
         We are kin with all Earth beings.
         We celebrate the mystery!
         We are connected to that ultimate Mystery,
         the Impulse behind all birth on Earth.

Blessing

LEADER   I now invite you to share a blessing with each other. Face the person
         next to you, join hands, feel the soil on each other's hands, and
         repeat the blessing after me.

May the embrace of our Mother Earth,

who unites us all in mystery,

move us to embrace and care for

all our kindred Earth beings,

whose orange clay and breath from God

we share in this our planet home.

A Sacred Site on the Rocks

The Mystery of Wonder

The Setting

Participants gather round the **Earth bowl** in which rests a fossil that is
either embedded in a rock or whose markings are captured by the shape of
the rock. The fossil is a symbol of wonder embedded in nature.

And/Or

Participants gather, whether in physical space or in the imagination of their
consciousness, on high rocks and look out to sea, across mountains, or up
into the sky. They become conscious of the wonder that moves mind and
spirit. They relive the experience of wonder that Job encounters when confronted by God from the whirlwind. They await the moment of awe in the
face of Wonder emerging from the wonders before them.

The Voice from the Whirlwind

LEADER   Listen now to the voice of God from the whirlwind, a voice that
          once addressed Job and that now addresses you, confronting you
          with the wonders of nature. Pause after each voice from God and
          wonder!

VOICE 1   Behold the wonder of Earth! Were you there when she evolved, on
          the day her foundations were laid and the galaxies sang? Can you
          sense how the cosmos celebrated when Earth came alive? Can you
          comprehend this wonder called Earth?

VOICE 2   Behold the wonder of the oceans! Can you grasp the laws that limit
          her flows across the shores? Can you appreciate that from space the
          shoreline is like a playpen that keeps this child in check? Do you
          realise that ocean waters circulate through your body and mine?

VOICE 3 Behold the wonder of light! Can you discover the origins of light hidden in the darkness at the beginning of time? Are you able to imagine the explosion of light as the forces of the cosmos burst into view? Do you wonder at the light that flows from a now extinct supernova?

VOICE 1 Behold the wonder of stars! Since you are wise in this world, can you understand how the constellations travel endlessly through space? Have you mastered the celestial laws that govern movements in the heavens? Could you imagine applying these laws to rebalance the disorders on Earth?

VOICE 2 Behold the wonder of weather! Does the mystery of thunderstorms bringing rain to arid land lift your spirits? Do you understand the way dewdrops and hoarfrost enter the atmosphere? Does the complexity of the climatic system keep you guessing?

VOICE 3 Behold the wonder of the deeps! Do you have any grasp of the domains still far beyond any of our knowledge? Can you imagine the deeps of space, whether they be black holes or super stars? Are you ready to explore darkness and death?

VOICE 1 The wonder of clouds! Do you sense the mystery of clouds that produce floods of water and flashes of lightning? Can you discern the amazing mystery that wisdom is imbedded in their being, guiding them to provide the moisture needed for life on Earth? And will you celebrate mystery with cumulus clouds?

Exploring Mystery

LEADER We now explore the mystery of wonder in nature and the spiritual Wonder deep in Earth.

VOICE 1   Do you sense mystery
in the wonders of the universe,
from the ocean depths to the distant stars?

VOICE 2   And in the wonders of the weather,
the sudden laughter of lightning
and the hidden wisdom in the clouds?

VOICE 1   Do you sense mystery
in the wonders of the wild,
from the wise ant to the enigmatic ostrich?

VOICE 2   And in the crystals encased in rock,
the perplexing fossils of ancient species,
and the emergence of life from volcanoes?

VOICE 1   Do you sense the spiritual in
the Wonder that provokes all wonder?

VOICE 2   The wonder of our world is indeed sacred,
the mystery of Wonder evoking wonder
in us and all of creation.

Memories of Wonder

LEADER   We pause now to share memories of wonder, moments when a wonder amazed us or the Wonder of all wonders was revealed to us through a wonder.

Memory of a Sacred Rock

I stood on a hill at sunset
overlooking a massive rock;
a mile high, some say,
and twenty miles around.

The rock was Uluru,
a golden boulder rising from deep in the red centre of Australia,
a sacred site of Aboriginal peoples.
As I watched, the rock exuded wonder,
changing colour from instant to instant,
from celestial gold to earthy orange,
from vivid bronze to blazing red,
all the colours of a desert rainbow.

I sensed what many had sensed in other lands before me,
that point of spiritual concentration,
the navel of Earth
where spirit is incarnate in the soil
and the intrinsic worth of Earth is revealed.
Wonder in a rock
and in my consciousness.

Symbolic Action: Sharing Wonder

LEADER   You are now invited to approach the Earth bowl,
take the fossil from the bowl.
Feel its texture, discern its beauty, sense its mystery,
and then hand it to the person next to you.
(*Participants run their hands over the fossil in silent meditation and pass the fossil slowly around while the leader reads the reflection.*)

LEADER   Reflect for a moment on the mystery of this fossil,
this wonder in your hands.
Thousands of years ago this creature was alive,
its body pulsing with life and energy.
At some point in the distant past
this creature was encased in matter,
whether on the deep sea floor,
in volcanic lava,
or in the sands of the desert.
And the creature became one with rock.
The rock in turn preserved its form,
its identity, the wonder of its nature,
more precious even than gold.
We hold in our hands a wonder
from a world of wonders
in which our consciousness can discern
the Wonder of all wonders.

Blessing

LEADER   I now invite you to share a blessing with each other. Face the person
next to you and repeat the blessing after me.

May the wonders of this world
stun you with their splendour
until you appreciate
that their goodness is richer than gold
and ought to be preserved
as sacred treasure.
They are the original artwork of evolution,
and the fingers of God.

Sacred Site in a Forest

The Mystery of Life

The Setting

Participants gather round the **Earth bowl** which contains sprigs of rosemary and/or eucalyptus leaves (or whatever is available). These green plants are symbols of the pulse of Life in all living things.

And/Or

Participants gather, whether in physical space or in the imagination of their consciousness, beside a stream in a forest rich with green flora. They become conscious of the deep Impulse that brings life to all in sight. In their hands they hold a branch of eucalyptus leaves or a sprig of rosemary.

Celebrating with the Psalmist (Psalm 104)

LEADER   Sky life! Amazing!
A living Presence fills the sky
like a wild and wondrous night rider!

**PEOPLE   You make the clouds your chariot!
You ride on the wings of the wind!
You make the winds your messengers!
Fire and flame your ministers!**

LEADER   Bird life! Amazing!
A deep impulse causes the rivers to flow
and the birds of the air to celebrate!

**PEOPLE   You make springs gush forth in the valleys!
They flow between the hills!
By the streams the birds have their habitations!
They sing among the branches!**

LEADER   Plant life! Amazing!
A life impulse in the ground
creates plants to sustain and celebrate!

**PEOPLE   You cause the grass to grow for the cattle
and make plants for people to cultivate,
to bring forth food from the Earth,
and wine to gladden the human heart,
oil to make the face shine,
and bread to strengthen the human heart.**

LEADER   Tree life! Amazing!
Trees are planted, watered, and nurtured
personally by a true tree lover.

PEOPLE   The trees of the Lord are watered abundantly!
          The cedars of Lebanon that God planted!
          In them the birds build their nests!
          The stork has its home in the fir trees!

LEADER   Sea life! Amazing!

PEOPLE   Yonder is the sea, great and wide!
          Creeping things innumerable are there!
          There go the ships!
          And Leviathan that you created to play with!

LEADER   Land life! Amazing!

PEOPLE   When you hide your face they are dismayed!
          When you take away their breath they die!
          When you sent forth your breath, they are created!
          And you renew the face of the ground!

LEADER   All life! Celebrate!

PEOPLE   May the Presence of the Lord last forever!
          May the Lord celebrate the Lord's works!

Earth Memories

LEADER   Return to your childhood for a moment. Be a child again! What
          are your earliest memories of where you lived and played? Are there
          spots outside your home that were special, where you felt the pulse of
          life? Are there places or images that evoked the mystery of life?
          (*Participants reflect on locations where nature was alive in their past.*)

My Memory of the Breath of God

Time and again as a boy
I wandered through the bush,
caressing the green moss on myrtles hundreds of years old,
tasting the soft gum of blooming wattles,
smelling the aroma of crushed eucalyptus leaves,
hearing country music in the surrounding air.
Then one day, as if by revelation,
what I was reading about God's spirit came to life.
I breathed in time with the trees,
in tune with the breeze,
inhaling deeply.
I was breathing the breath of God,
as Adam had done in the forest of Eden.
The air, the wind,
the atmosphere
were the very breath of God, the Spirit
that animates me and every tree in every age.
I was in Eden.

Symbolic Action: Sensing the Pulse

LEADER   You are invited now to take your sprig of rosemary or some eucalyptus leaves to stimulate our senses as we seek to reconnect with that mystery called Life.

Seeing

We focus our eyes on the leaves in our hand; their shape, their texture, their colour, their inner power – the living impulse that inspires plants to grow from Earth.
(Participants focus their eyes on their leaves for a brief time.)

PEOPLE   **Earth, help us see the deep impulse revealed**
in the life of this plant here and now.

Hearing

LEADER   We brush the leaves across an ear and hear the sounds, the song they make as they touch our skin, our mind, our spirit.
(Participants brush the leaves past their ears a few times.)

PEOPLE   **Earth, help us to hear the spirit within,**
breathing life into us through this plant
and all the plants of Earth.

Touch

LEADER   We feel the leaves between our fingers, their textures, their skin, their rough stems – green life forms made of Earth.
(Participants feel the leaves between their fingers.)

PEOPLE   **Earth, help us discern the wisdom of this plant,**
the mystery that makes a rosemary a rosemary,
and a eucalypt a eucalypt.

Smell

LEADER   We crush a few leaves and smell their soul;
the aroma from the plant penetrates our souls.
(Participants crush a few leaves and smell the aroma.)

PEOPLE   **Earth, help us, through this aroma, to sense Presence**
evoking Presence among us.

Taste

LEADER We take a few crushed leaves and taste them, savour the rich flavour,
a gourmet gift to celebrate life.
(Participants taste and savour a few leaves.)

PEOPLE **Earth, help us to celebrate this plant,**
to celebrate all life on Earth,
and celebrate life itself as it pulses through us.

Blessing

LEADER I now invite you to share a blessing with each other. Face the person
next to you and repeat the blessing after me.

May the atmosphere,

the moist breath of God enveloping us,

penetrate every pore of our planet

and activate all those impulses needed

to keep our forests green,

our swallows singing,

and our dragonflies dancing.

Scorched Earth Sites

The Mystery of Voice

The Setting

Participants gather round the **Earth bowl** which contains a burnt branch, a chain from a chainsaw, a handful of waste, a picture of a degraded coral reef, a can marked as poison, an empty nest, and a green sprout from a tree or bush. These items are symbols of scorched Earth sites across the planet.

And/Or

Participants gather, whether in physical space or in the imagination of their consciousness, at a location where the seven scorched Earth sites are represented. Earth's voice speaks at each site and reminds us of her suffering because of acts of human destruction.

The Voices of Earth

LEADER   We gather beside this burnt branch – a scorched memorial – to hear the voice of Earth crying. This memorial remembers scorched Earth sites where fierce bushfires raged in recent years.

EARTH – VOICE 1 *(holding up a burnt branch)*

       This site is a hot spot among many on my landscape,
       a spot made hot by human acts of greed.
       A bushfire lit by humans scorched my face.

A hurricane of flames destroyed a million blue wrens,
and melted koalas, cockatoos, and dingoes,
as the gases from clusters of eucalypts exploded
and balls of fires spun from one hill to another,
leaving me screaming in pain, seared and angry.
Can you hear me?

PEOPLE   **We hear you. And we feel your pain.**

LEADER   We gather beside this old tree stump – a scorched Earth memorial – to hear the voice of Earth crying. This memorial remembers
scorched Earth sites where old growth forests have been decimated
by human greed.

EARTH – VOICE 2 *(holding up a chain from a chainsaw)*

This site is where once an ancient forest thrived,
a dense mass of living wood many hundreds of years old.
Canopy and undergrowth I nurtured as
the lungs and laughter of the planet,
a domain of dancing creatures,
birds, bees, and blossoms,
until chainsaws silenced it all
and left me groaning deep within.
Can you hear me?

PEOPLE   **We hear you. And we feel your pain.**

LEADER   We gather beside this hole filled with waste – a scorched Earth
memorial – to hear the voice of Earth crying. This site remembers
scorched Earth locations where nuclear explosions, waste, and
leaks have killed through radioactivity.

EARTH – VOICE 3 *(holding up a handful of waste)*

> This site is where Earth beings once lived,
> where grass was green and souls ran free.
> Ego-led humans took uranium from my soul
> and turned it into radioactive evil
> shattering life and land.
> This is a wasteland, a scorched Earth site,
> that wounds my spirit
> and leaves my soul longing for peace.
> Can you hear me?

PEOPLE   **We hear you. And we feel your pain.**

LEADER   We gather beside this well – a scorched Earth memorial – to hear the voice of Earth crying from below. This site remembers scorched Earth locations where Aboriginal people were poisoned or massacred by colonial invaders.

EARTH – VOICE 4 *(holding up a can marked as poison)*

> This site is where my custodians, my kin,
> my children who emerged from my womb,
> Aboriginal peoples who tended my body,
> heard my voice and sensed my spirit.
> This is also where they were poisoned at wells,
> thrown off cliffs,
> and massacred as vermin in the paddocks
> by white fellas unwilling to honour my children.
> Can you hear me?

PEOPLE   **We hear you. And we feel your pain.**

Leader   We gather beside this polluted reef – a scorched Earth memorial – to hear the voice of Earth crying. This site remembers scorched Earth locations in the seas and rivers where poisonous waste defiles the ecosystems and global warming causes the degradation of coral reefs.

Earth – Voice 5 *(holding up a picture of a degraded reef)*

This site is where humans
have violated the ocean ecosystem,
where industry has disposed of its ugly waste
and circulating currents have accumulated plastic islands;
global warming has burnt off coral reefs
and the rhythms of life and nurture
have been transformed into death traps
for living creatures of the deep.
Can you hear me?

People   **We hear you. And we feel your pain.**

Leader   We gather beside this empty bird's nest – a scorched Earth memorial – to hear the voice of Earth crying from below. This site remembers scorched Earth locations across the landscape where species have become extinct because of global warming or the irresponsible destruction of habitat.

Earth – Voice 6 *(holding up an empty bird's nest)*

This site is where my green vegetation
nurtured masses of birds, bats, and butterflies,
shimmering grasses, rushes, and ferns,
fragile animals that inhabit the ground.
Here they loved me with their songs
until a horde of humans
stole their home and left them to die.
Can you hear me?

PEOPLE   **We hear you. And we feel your pain.**

LEADER   We gather beside this green shoot – a scorched Earth memorial
          – to hear the voice of Earth crying. This site remembers scorched
          Earth locations across the planet that Earth is rejuvenating.

EARTH – VOICE 7 *(holding up a green shoot)*

          This site is where lightning struck and scorched the Earth
          (whether lightning from my skies or human hands),
          and where now I nurture again the green shoots of life
          that rise from my groaning heart
          as reminders to my human children
          to reverse all scorched practices
          and join with me in greening the planet
          to be a healthy habitat once again.
          Can you hear me?

PEOPLE   **We hear you. And we feel your pain.**

Symbolic Action: A Memorial

LEADER   You are invited now to erect a memorial to a site on Mother Earth
          that has been scorched by human violence, greed, ignorance,
          and disdain. Any one of the scorched Earth sites above might be
          considered. We begin with places where creatures of the sea have
          been sacrificed and invite your contribution.

WHERE: Where might we erect such a memorial? On the beach opposite
          the Great Barrier Reef in Queensland or on the shoreline near New
          Orleans in Louisiana?

SACRIFICE: How might we characterise the nature of the sacrifice being
          remembered in the memorial?

NAMES: What creatures might we name as having been sacrificed?

DEDICATION: How might we word the dedication, remembering Earth as the mother of those creatures sacrificed?
(Participants may then create a draft memorial and place it on the Earth bowl or at an appropriate location for the public to see.)

Blessing

LEADER I now invite you to share a blessing with each other. Face the person next to you and repeat the blessing after me.

May the groaning of creation,

deep and blue and bold,

penetrate our smothered consciousness,

until we become prophets of Earth,

giving voice to her injustices

and supporting her spirit.

A Sacred Site in a Garden

The Mystery of Wisdom

Setting

Participants gather round the **Earth bowl** in which rests an enclosed ant's nest (or facsimile). The mystery of wisdom in nature is here exemplified by ants, recalling the proverb: Consider the way of the ant and be wise.

And/Or

Participants gather, whether in a physical space or in the imagination of their consciousness, in the bush or in a garden where ants and bees, butterflies and flowers are interacting. There, they seek to discern the wisdom imbedded in nature that governs the mysteries they see. In the reading below, after each response, the leader may pause to allow others to add their own examples of wisdom in nature appropriate to the category.

The Source of Wisdom

LEADER   Where can we find wisdom?

PEOPLE   **Where is her place on our planet?**

LEADER   Where did the wise of old find wisdom?

PEOPLE   **In the way of the ant gathering grain for winter!**
In the way of the bee amassing honey in a hive!
In the way of the eagle soaring high in the sky!

LEADER   Where do nature-lovers find wisdom?

PEOPLE   **In the impulse of birds gathering at dawn to cross the ocean!**

In the impulse of bats flying blind in the evening sky!
In the impulse of salmon surging upstream to spawn!

LEADER   Where do the scientists find wisdom?

PEOPLE   **In the information encoded in the genes of the body!**
In the information imbedded in the cells of the brain!
In the information shared by an embryo in the womb!

LEADER   Where do the evolutionists find wisdom?

PEOPLE   **In the mystery of mindless matter evolving into mind!**
In the mystery of cosmic dust evolving into consciousness!
In the mystery of lifeless elements evolving into elephants!

LEADER   Where does God find wisdom?

PEOPLE   **In the laws of nature that govern changes in climate!**
In the laws of nature that guide flashes of lightning!
In the laws of nature that control the currents at sea!

LEADER   And where do you find wisdom personally as you reflect on the mysteries of nature around you?

Participants are invited to respond by relating experiences from their own world that express an awareness of this spiritual dimension of nature called wisdom.

Memories of Wisdom

LEADER   We pause now to share memories of wisdom, moments when the mystery of wisdom implanted in nature was revealed to us through the rhythms and laws of nature.

A Memory from New Zealand

I sat on the shore of a bay in Auckland. Around me hundreds of bar-tailed godwits had gathered from points all around the island. All day they raced round in a frenzy of feeding. Suddenly, as if a signal was heard from within each of them, they all began to circle and form a spiral of spinning life. Slowly the spiral swirled out to sea and the godwits were on their way to Alaska to feed and breed.

At that moment
I could sense wisdom,
the wisdom of flight,
and the wisdom of memory
encoded in their spirit.
I was conscious of the amazing intelligence
of fellow Earth beings,
guiding themselves non-stop
across the vast ocean to a place
more than ten thousand kilometres away!

And I was humbled.

Symbolic Action: Sharing Wisdom

LEADER   We are now invited to hold an ant
or watch an ant closely and reflect
on the mystery of wisdom in the ant
and in all of nature around us.

VOICE 1   Consider the senses of the ant!
          Can you discern how the ant knows with such certainty
          where to travel so rapidly on such tiny legs?

PEOPLE   **The ant, like every tiny creature,**
          has an inner code, a blueprint
          that governs its way of living,
          a blueprint the wise have named wisdom.

VOICE 2   Consider the eggs of the ant!
          Can you sense the amazing capacity
          of an ant to create community?

PEOPLE   **The genes within the ant eggs**
          have deep wisdom codes
          that enable the mysteries of birth
          and nurture to happen in their nests.

VOICE 1   Consider the antennae of the ant!
          Can you fathom how the ant knows
          when and where to gather food?

PEOPLE   **That wisdom reaches deeper**
          into the mysterious blueprint
          that guided the evolution of Earth
          and the emergence of mind.

VOICE 2   Consider the mind of the ant.
          Can you discern how the ant communicates
          with every ant it meets along the path?

PEOPLE   **From the mind of the ant**
          to mind in all matter,
          we wonder about the depth of wisdom.

Voice 1   Consider the world of the ant!
Can you grasp how seemingly helpless insects
survive in all domains of this planet?

People   **From the rhythms of Earth's currents
to the balance of Earth's climate,
we wonder about the ways of wisdom
imbedded in the deeps of nature.**

Voice 2   Consider the ethics of an ant!
Can you discern how ants willingly share
without enforcement by strong leaders or written laws ?

People   **From our ignorance about wisdom in nature
to the folly of upsetting nature's balance,
we wonder where wisdom is found among humans!**

Leader   Let us follow the lead of the Sage,
and discern the ways of Wisdom in nature.
Let us find the wisdom needed to sustain our planet.

Blessing

Leader   I now invite you to share a blessing with each other. Face the person
next to you and repeat the blessing after me.

May the ways of wisdom,

imbedded in the codes and laws of nature,

confront our consciousness

so that we recognize, celebrate, and sustain

the mystery of the blueprint that sustains us

and informs the incredible impulses

deep within the ecosystems of our planet.

A Sacred Site in the Wild

The Mystery of Compassion

The Setting

Participants gather round the **Earth bowl** in which rests a replica of a delicate bird's nest lined with wool; there are several (replica) bird's eggs in the nest. The nest is a symbol of compassion and caring among Earth beings such as birds. It points to the mystery of compassion in the cosmos.

And/Or

Participants gather, whether in physical space or in the imagination of their consciousness, in the wild where an elephant is caring for an orphaned newborn. They become conscious of compassion as a mystery even in the wild.

Searching the Mystery

LEADER   Where might we sense compassion in the cosmos?
          Where might we find empathy in nature?

VOICE 1   What if we search for compassion among the microbes and cells when they strive to become new life forms?

What if we discern compassion as an integral component of evolution?

VOICE 2   What if we search for soul in the core of creation where the forces of gravity govern galaxies spinning through time?
What if we discern soul in space?

VOICE 3   What if we search for empathy in the depths of the jungle where carnivores rage and reptiles are rife?
What if we could discern empathy in the wild?

VOICE 1   Can you accept the possibility that there is a Compassionate Force (perhaps called God) moving all domains of nature to nurture as well as survival?
Can you accept love as an agent of survival?

VOICE 2   Can you identify with a God who suffers with all creatures through the natural disasters and cosmic explosions of our world?
Can you sense God deep in the erupting volcano?

VOICE 3   Could you ever accept a crucified God, a compassionate power that is ready to suffer humiliation at the hands of humans to expose that inner dimension of the cosmos we call love?
Yes, does the cosmos have soul?

Memories of Compassion in Nature

LEADER   Let us now share our experiences of compassion in nature, whether they are among animals, birds, small creatures, flora, or unseen forces. Let us disclose the mystery of empathy in the non-human world around us. Did you discover a suffering God or a cosmic Christ in your experience of nature?
(Participants share, slowly and quietly, as their inner selves move them.)

Earth Compassion

Many who explore the evolution
of my mother Earth
tend to see a battleground,
the survival of the fiercest in
a dog-eat-dog world.

My sympathy
is with those new scientists
who discern the survival of the caring,
the web of compassion
that creates community
and integrates ecosystems.
Can I trust their views?

And Earth, some would argue,
is part of that community
communicating concern
from species to species
and from the depths to the heights.
Can I discern such a mystery?

Then one frightening day,
I sensed something in the tsunami
that flooded islands of the Pacific
and inundated Indian Ocean shores.

The groaning of Earth,
the dangerous dislocations,
were not just selfish quaking
but a message of empathy to all creatures,
a caring cry
that some Earth beings heard
and then left for higher ground,
like the elephants in Sri Lanka
and the reptiles of Acer.

Sad to say,
most of the Earth beings called humans
were not listening
and so did not sense Earth's compassion.

Reflection

LEADER   Compassion, were you there?

VOICE   **I was there. I was there.**

LEADER   Were you there when the oil spill reached the shore?

VOICE   **I was there with the birds on the beach.**

LEADER   Were you there when they tested atomic bombs?

VOICE   **I was there in the radioactive soil.**

LEADER   Were you there when fires swept through the trees?

VOICE   **I was there with the koalas in the branches.**

LEADER   Were you there when the potato famine struck?

VOICE   **I was there with babies dying of hunger.**

LEADER   Were you there when they fought the First World War?

VOICE   **I was there with the wounded, both horse and rider.**

LEADER   Were you there when they crucified my Lord?

VOICE   **I was there on the cross. I was there.**

Symbolic Action: Sharing Compassion

LEADER   You are invited now to take the bird's nest in your hands, remove a tiny fibre of grass or wool as a token of the whole nest and the mystery of compassion in nature.

What does the delicate and gentle building of this nest suggest to you?
(Participants hold the fibres of the nest, observe its intricate form, and respond.)
What does the soft wool lining of the nest imply for you?
(Participants hold the fibres of the nest, observe their softness, and respond.)
What does this nest imply about the heart and hope of this bird?
(Participants hold the fibres of the nest, imagine the mother on the nest, and respond.)
Can you sense from this bird and this nest that nature has soul and/or there is compassion in the cosmos?
(Participants hold the fibres of the nest and respond.)

Blessing

LEADER   I now invite you to share a blessing with each other. Face the person next to you and repeat the blessing after me.

May the compassion of the cosmos

and the empathy of Earth

stir within you a consciousness

of a spiritual force in nature

that shares pain,

heals hearts,

and nurtures hope.

BIBLIOGRAPHY

Berry, Thomas. *The Great Work: Our Way into the Future.* New York: Bell Tower, 1999.

Brown, William. *The Seven Pillars of Creation: The Bible, Science and the Ecology of Wonder.* New York: Oxford University Press, 2010.

Cowley, Joy. "The Way of the Cross." *Tui Motu InterIslands Monthly Independent Catholic Magazine*, April 2011.

Dell, Katharine. "The Significance of the Wisdom Tradition in the Ecological Debate." David Horrell (ed.). *Ecological Hermeneutics: Biblical, Historical and Theological Perspectives.* London: Barnes and Noble, 2010.

Duroux, Mary. *Dirge for Hidden Art.* Moruya: Heritage Publishing, 1992.

Earth Bible Team. "The Voice of Earth: More than Metaphor?" Norman Habel. *The Earth Story in the Psalms and the Prophets: The Earth Bible Volume Four.* Sheffield: Sheffield Academic Press, 2001.

Eco, Umberto. *Kant and the Platypus: Essays on Language and Cognition.* London: Vintage, 2000.

Edwards, Denis. *Jesus, the Wisdom of God: An Ecological Theology.* Homebush, Sydney: St Pauls, 1995.

—— *The God of Evolution.* New York: Paulist Press, 1999.

Fejo, Wally. "The Voice of the Earth: An Indigenous Reading of Genesis 9." Norman Habel. *The Earth Story in Genesis: The Earth Bible Volume Two.* Sheffield: Sheffield Academic Press, 2000.

Flannery, Tim. *Here on Earth. An Argument for Hope.* Melbourne: Text Publishing, 2010.

Geering, Lloyd. *Coming Back to Earth: From Gods, to God, to Gaia.* Salem, Oregon: Polebridge, 2009.

Habel, Norman. *Reconciliation. Searching for Australia's Soul.* Sydney: Harper-Collins, 1999.

——"Is the Wild Ox Willing to Serve You? Challenging the Mandate to Dominate." Habel, Norman and Shirley Wurst (ed.). *The Earth Story in Wisdom Traditions: The Earth Bible Volume Three.* Sheffield: Sheffield Academic Press, 2001.

——"The Implications of God Discovering Wisdom in Earth.": *Cognition in Context.* Van Wolde, Ellen (ed.). *Job 28.* Leiden: Brill, 2003.

——and Peter Trudinger, (ed.). *Exploring Ecological Hermeneutics.* Atlanta: SBL, 2008.

—— *An Inconvenient Text. Is a Green Reading of the Bible Possible?* Adelaide: ATF Press, 2009.

—— *The Birth, the Curse and the Greening of Earth: An Ecological Reading of Genesis 1–11.* Sheffield: Sheffield Phoenix, 2011.

Hall, Stephen. *Wisdom: From Philosophy to Neuroscience.* St Lucia: University of Queensland Press, 2010.

Hiebert, Theodore. "Air, the First Sacred Thing: The Conception of *ruach* in the Hebrew Scriptures." Habel, Norman and Peter Trudinger (eds.). *Exploring Ecological Hermeneutics.* SBL Symposium, Atlanta: SBL, 2008.

Keen, Sam. *Apology for Wonder.* New York: Harper and Row, 1969.

Lovelock, James. *The Revenge of Gaia.* London: Allen Lane, 2006.

Macy, Joanna and John Seed. "Gaia Meditations." Gottlieb, Rogers S. (ed.) *This Sacred Earth: Religion, Nature Environment.* New York: Routledge, 1996.

Nelson, Kevin. *The God Impulse: Is Religion Hardwired into the Brain?* London: Simon & Schuster, 2011.

Rainbow Spirit Elders. *Rainbow Spirit Theology: Towards an Australian Aboriginal Theology.* Blackburn: HarperCollins, 1997.

Report of the Commission of Theology and Church Relations: The Lutheran Church – Missouri Synod. *Together with All Creatures: Caring for God's Living Earth.* St Louis: Lutheran Church – Missouri Synod, 2010.

Sanguin, Bruce. *Darwin, Divinity and the Dance of the Cosmos.* Kelowna, B.C.: CopperHouse, 2007.

Spong, John Shelby. *Eternal Life: A New Vision Beyond Religion, Beyond Theism, Beyond Heaven and Hell.* New York: HarperOne, 2009.

Suzuki, David and Amanda McConnell. *The Sacred Balance: Rediscovering Our Place in Nature.* London: Bantam, 1997.

——and Kathy Vanderlinden. *You Are the Earth.* Sydney: Allen and Unwin, 1999.

Webb, Val. *Stepping Out with the Sacred: Human Attempts to Engage the Divine.* London: Continuum, 2010.

Wurst, Shirley (Joh) "Retrieving Earth's Voice in Jeremiah: An Annotated Voicing of Jeremiah 4." Habel, Norman. *The Earth Story in the Psalms and the Prophets. The Earth Bible Volume Two.* Sheffield: Sheffield Academic Press, 2001.

Yunupingu, G. "Concepts of Land and Spirituality." Patel-Gray, A. (ed.). *Aboriginal Spirituality, Present and Future.* Melbourne: HarperCollins, 1996.

INDEX

A

abad...73
Adam 55
adamah..55
adoption
    by church 61, 68
    in baptism...................................60
ant 142
atmosphere 100, 103, 115
    breath of God 99, 100
Australia War Memorial 135

B

baptism.................................60, 62, 103
Berry, Thomas..............42, 45, 127, 130
bildende Kraft................................142
birth
    as mystery 67
    mystery of..................................59
    of Earth 58
    unclean 60
blue...120
breath
    atmosphere................................99
    of God 99, 115, 116
bushfires..158

C

chesed 166
Christ
    cosmic......................................170
Colossians
    1:19–20..........................169, 170
compassion
    and God 165, 166, 169, 177
    cosmic Christ...........................170
    covenant with...........................178

definition 164
Eucharist 169
impulse to nurture.....................171, 173
in evolution......................................171
in my tradition 169
in nature 164, 165, 170, 174
in the Scriptures.......................165, 167
Jesus 167
life impulse 164, 179
of Earth 175
presence 164, 178
soul 164
spiritual force...................................177
voice 164, 179
wisdom.....................................164, 180
wonder 179
consciousness
    human 107
    spiritual 107
covenant
    and compassion 178
    as Earth being............................73
    presence 49
    to partner with Earth 74
    with Earth........................93, 136
    with life 115
    with wonder 94
Cowley, Joy 108
creation
    fallen................................84, 85
    larvae Dei 41
    Luthor......................................41

D

deep

    voice of the 120

Dell, Katharine 149

derek 141, 143, 147

    technical sense 141

Duroux, Mary 129

E

Earth

    and compassion 170

    as mother 57, 67, 68, 74

    as resource 63, 83

    as womb 56

    biological parent 62

    birth of 58, 67

    caring for 73

    covenant 93, 136

    home 69

    sacred connection with 70, 73

    suffers 123, 125, 128, 136

    transient 84

    under threat 93

    voice of 134

    womb 67

Earth being 54, 73

    in my tradition 60

    interconnected 64, 66, 69, 74, 86

    my life as 68

    superior 63

Ecclesiastes

    3:19–21 102

ecology 47

Edwards, Denis 108, 169

Ephesians

    1:10 170

    2 169

Exodus

    16:10 35

    24:15–18 36

    24:34–38 36

    33:17–23 38

F

Fejo, Wally 126

Fire of El 44

Flannery, Tim 172

flood 84, 120, 126, 167

forest 56

Frye, Stephen 174

G

Geering, Lloyd 65

Genesis

    1:1–13 .... 58, 79

    1:27–28 64

    2 .... 55, 66, 73

    2:5, 15 74

    2:15 55

    3 56

    6:5–8 167

    7:22 56

    8:21 84

God
adoptive parent 61
and compassion 165, 166, 169, 173
and wisdom 144, 146, 155, 160
and wonder 79
backside of 38
breath of.... 56, 57, 99, 100, 103, 104, 108, 115
face of 38
in heaven 39, 40, 60, 68
presence 35–37, 40, 46, 52, 82, 134
gold 79

H

heaven
eternal 84
Hebrews
11:13–16 105
Hiebert, Theodore 99

I

I Corinthians
15:51–54 104
I Kings
8:10–11 36
8:27 36
19:11–13 46
imago Dei 63
impulse
spiritual 72
Isaiah
6 34

J

Jeremiah
4:19–28 121
12:11 119
Jesus 41
and compassion 167
eternal life 104
Wisdom's child 152
Job
1:1–3 80
1:12 56
1:21 53
12:13–15 80
28 .... 144, 150, 160
28:12 139
28:23–24 144
28:23–27 160
38 79
42:1–6 82
John
1:4 104
1:14 41

K

kabash 64
kabod 35
Keen, Sam 92
kochma 146

L

law of love 172
Leviathan 101
life
    after death 60
    and nature 102
    and play 101
    and spirit 98
    and wisdom 102
    as celebration 100, 113
    breath of God 101
    common origin 65
    connected 106
    emergence 105, 108
    eternal 85, 102–104, 106, 117
    green mystery 98
    impulse 72, 117
    impulse, compassion 164
    in my tradition 103
    in nature 105, 116
    spirit of, and nature 110
life impulse 109
logos 150, 176
Lovelock, James 153
Luther, Martin 72
Luther Standing Bear 67

M

MacLeish, Archibald 41
maqom 144
Maralinga 128, 131
Matthew
    11:19 152
    13:44–45 152
McConnell, Amanda 172

Moses 36, 37, 46
mystery
    breath 99
    green 98
    intrinsic worth 82
    of life 74
    of presence in nature 34
    of voice 137
    voice 120, 128, 134
    wisdom 82, 140, 150
    wonder 80

N

nature
    text of 42
Nelson, Kevin 107
nephesh 166

O

orange 54, 73, 100
    mystery 56
original sin 60, 62, 63, 67, 84

P

place
    breaking of boundaries 158
    in nature 158
presence
    and Earth 130
    and wonder 89, 96
    compassion 164
    everywhere 36, 37, 39, 40, 43, 48
    God's 37, 38
    in church 41
    in my tradition 39

in my world...45
in nature 38–40, 42, 46, 50, 51
in primal stillness...................................47
in stillness..47
in the Scriptures....................................34
in wisdom.. 161
mystery of..34
permeating...51
red 43
sacred 45, 52
spiritual 34
sustaining mystery of 48, 51
visible 35–37
primal
   world 55
Proverbs
   3:18 102
   3:19 148
   4:23..97
   6:6–8 142
   8... 150
   8:22–31 146
   8:35 102
   16:22 102
   30:18..77
Psalm
   19:1 44
   19:2–4 44
   23... 165
   33:5 166
   39...57
   65:12–13 123
   104... 100
   139:13–15 57
   193:7 33

Q
qana.. 146
R
rada 64, 73
rainbow spirit 75, 128
rapture..84
Romans
   8:19–25... 123
ruach...99
S
sacrament
   baptism.................................60, 62, 103
   Eucharist... 169
   Holy Communion 41
Saint Paul.. 104
salvation..40
sanctus..35
Sanguin, Bruce.......................50, 86, 105, 152
satan...41
seraphim.............................35, 36, 39, 40, 48
spirit
   mystery of..99
spirit 54
   holy, and evolution 108
   presence of 109
Spong, John Shelby.................................... 114
stillness...46
   primal 47
   suspended in............................. 45, 46, 51
stolen generation 174
sunset 43, 50, 52
Suzuki, David 65, 67, 98, 106, 127, 172, 173

U

Uluru...78, 89

V

Vanderlinden, Kathy.....................................65
violet...165
voice
    as metaphor...............................123, 125
    compassion..164
    hearing Earth........................ 134, 135, 137
    in my tradition.....................................125
    in nature.................120, 127, 131, 136, 137
    in Scripture..121
    mystery of............................. 120, 128, 137
    of Earth..........120, 123–125, 128, 133, 134

W

way..141, 143
    technical sense....................................141
Webb, Val...78, 87
wisdom
    and creation.......................... 145, 147, 148
    and God..........................148, 149, 155, 160
    as mystery.............................140, 150, 176
    as sacrament..161
    as the way..147
    compassion..164
    covenant...159
    definition...140
    elephants..150
    fairy penguins......................................150
    human..149
    inate. See derek or way
    in my tradition......................................149
    in my world...154

in nature................140, 149, 150, 158, 160
Jesus..152
literature...140
living force...155
mystery..82
place of.. 144, 145
wonder
    and evolution...86
    and gold...79
    and Presence.....................................89, 96
    and salvation...85
    as a journey..89
    clouds..82, 88
    deep, the..82, 88
    Earth.....................................80, 84, 87, 93
    in my tradition.......................................83
    in nature...............................77, 78, 89, 95
    light...81
    mystery..80, 95
    oceans..80
    of light..87
    of oceans..87
    react with..78, 96
    signs and..79
    spiritual..79
    stars..81, 88
    sustaining...92
    Uluru..89
    weather..81, 88
wonders
    seven..80

Y

Yunupingu..129, 135